Confucius

BLOOMSBURY GUIDES FOR THE PERPLEXED

Bloomsbury's Guides for the Perplexed are clear, concise and accessible introductions to thinkers, writers and subjects that students and readers can find especially challenging. Concentrating specifically on what it is that makes the subject difficult to grasp, these books explain and explore key themes and ideas, guiding the reader towards a thorough understanding of demanding material.

Bahá'í Faith: A Guide for the Perplexed, Robert H. Stockman
Kabbalah: A Guide for the Perplexed, Pinchas Giller
Mysticism: A Guide for the Perplexed, Paul Oliver
New Religious Movements: A Guide for the Perplexed, Paul Oliver
Zoroastrianism: A Guide for the Perplexed, Jenny Rose

Confucius

YONG HUANG

BLOOMSBURY

LONDON · NEW DELHI · NEW YORK · SYDNEY

PREFACE

There is no shortage of introductory books in English on Confucius or Confucianism, and so it seems a bit perplexing to add one, particularly in a series entitled "Guides for the Perplexed": When I teach Chinese philosophy in the United States, students often find Confucius and Confucianism (in comparison to other schools of thought such as Daoism and Buddhism, which may sound exotic and therefore perplexing) too bland to be interesting. What Confucius says, if not outright wrong, seems to be mostly common-sense platitudes.

So I decided to write this book in a slightly different way. The book is not written to satisfy people's curiosity about some archaic ideas of Confucius which are merely of historical interest. Instead I aim to show what Confucius can still teach us about our moral life in a contemporary (and, given the readership of this book, Western) world, despite the fact that he lived more than two and half millennia and half the globe apart from us. Thus, I do not follow the quite familiar practice of providing a systematic overview of Confucius's otherwise rather unsystematic concepts, such as humanity and propriety, superior persons and inferior persons, love and the golden rule, and knowledge and wisdom, as they appear in the *Analects*. Instead, with the exception of Chapter 1, which is about Confucius's life, in each chapter, I discuss one of his views which, while initially appearing perplexing, proves to be the most enlightening answer, or at least more enlightening than those found in Western philosophical traditions, to a question we have either in our everyday life or in our moral reflections. Or so I shall argue.

In Chapter 2, thus, I discuss Confucius's view about what to do with wrongdoers. In stark contrast to Jesus, who teaches us to turn the other cheek, or to use a phrase from the *Analects*, to return evil with a good turn, Confucius asks: if so, what do we return good with? Instead, Confucius teaches us to return good with good and return evil with uprightness. From the Christian viewpoint, the attitude that Jesus recommends is certainly more ideal and noble than Confucius's. Defenders of Confucius, in turn, often argue that Jesus's teaching is too idealistic to be practical, while Confucius was a moral realist. In this chapter, I argue that this is a misunderstanding. The main reason Confucius is against returning evil with a good turn is that it is not conducive to making the wrongdoer cease to be a wrongdoer, if it does not encourage the person to commit further wrongdoings. In Confucius's view, an upright person is one who is also inclined to make others upright. So when he asks us to return evil with uprightness, he is asking us to do what can make the wrongdoer cease to be a wrongdoer.

In Chapter 3, I discuss Confucius's answer to the question "why be moral (or virtuous)?" by exploring his view that one ought to love virtue as one loves sex. In Confucius's view, to be virtuous is a joyful thing. Of course, a person who asks the question "why be moral?," normally an egoist, may state that he or she cannot find joy, but instead can only find pain, in being moral. Confucius's response is that this is because they lack the relevant *virtuous* knowledge (not knowledge about virtue). Such knowledge requires not only the intellectual part of what is called *xin* 心 in Chinese (normally translated as heart-mind) but also its affective part, so that anyone who possesses such knowledge will be inclined to be moral and thus can take delight in being moral. The egoist may further ask: even if I can find joy in being moral, why do I have to find joy in being moral, as I can also find joy in being immoral? Confucius's answer is that being virtuous is a distinguishing mark of being human, and so anyone who is not virtuous is a defective human being.

In Chapter 4, I discuss the Socratic problem of whether virtue can be taught. Confucius's ethics is often regarded as a virtue ethics. However, one unique feature of Confucian virtue ethics, in comparison to virtue ethics familiar in the Western philosophical tradition, is that it avoids what Kantian critics call self-centeredness. For example, Aristotle makes it clear that a virtuous person is a genuine self-lover, a lover for his or her internal character, virtue, which is in contrast to the self-lover in a vulgar sense, a lover for his or her external well-being. While a virtuous person is concerned with both his or her own well-being and that of others, his or her own well-being in question is internal, while that of others in question is external. Since for Aristotle internal well-being is more important than external, a virtuous person is self-centered. Confucius, however, argues explicitly that a person cannot be regarded as virtuous unless he or she is inclined to help others be virtuous. The question then is how, since for Confucius virtue cannot be taught in the same way as intellectual knowledge or technical skills are taught. As virtue involves not only the intellectual aspect but also the affective part of *xin* (heart-mind), Confucius's answer is that the primary way to teach others to be virtuous is to morally move them by one's own exemplary virtuous actions.

In Chapter 5, I discuss Confucius's view about the appropriate attitude toward parents when they (are about to) commit wrongdoings. Since one of Confucius's famous, if not notorious, teachings is filial piety, which is often understood as to take care of and be obedient to one's parents, it is often understood that, for Confucius, we should connive at our parents' wrongdoings. This seems to be confirmed by one of the *Analects* passages, in which Confucius criticizes a boy with the name of being upright for bearing witness against his father stealing a sheep, saying that an upright son ought not to disclose his father's wrongdoing. However, I argue that, for Confucius, while a filial son of course ought to take care of his parents' well-being, it is more important to take care of their internal well-being than their external, especially when the two are in conflict. Since a parent, in committing a wrongdoing, definitely causes harm to his or her internal well-being, though benefitting externally, a filial son ought to remonstrate with his parent against the wrongdoing if it is not yet done, and for rectifying the wrongdoer as well as the wrongdoing, if it is already done. However, if so, why ought an upright son not disclose his parent's wrongdoing? Confucius's answer is that the atmosphere for the son to conduct effective remonstration will disappear if he discloses his parent's wrongdoing to the public or bears witness against his parent for the wrongdoing.

Thus, while this book is primarily intended for the general public, I also have in mind not only scholars interested in Chinese tradition but also moral philosophers in general. Throughout the book, I provide somewhat unconventional interpretations of several aspects of Confucius and make somewhat unfamiliar noises on a number of philosophical issues. In the former case, I not only make liberal use of Confucius's sayings both inside and outside the

Analects but also consult the extremely rich commentary tradition; in the case of the latter, I do my best to back up my claims by comparing them with alternative positions in terms of their respective strengths and weaknesses. While I do not claim that my interpretations of Confucius must be correct and my philosophical claims must be true, I do believe that they shed new light on some old materials and topics.

In the process of writing this book and developing the ideas presented therewith, I have accumulated huge debts to many friends and colleagues either through conversation with them or by reading their published works. While risking inevitable omissions, I do want to express my specific thanks to the following: Roger Ames, Yanmin An, Stephen Angle, John Berthrong, Lai Chen, Weigang Chen, Ted de Bary, Yiu-ming Fung, Paul Goldin, Qiyong Guo, Zhihong Hu, Thomas Hurka, P. J. Ivanhoe, Tao Jiang, Hwa Yol Jung, Kim-Chong Chong, Chenyang Li, Qingping Liu, Xiaogan Liu, On-cho Ng, Peimin Ni, Amy Olberding, Kwong-loi Shun, Jiyuan Yu, Vincent Shen, Michael Slote, Deborah Sommer, Justin Tiwald, Qingjie Wang, David Wong, Yang Xiao, and Guorong Yang.

Chapter 3 uses material from my "Confucius and Mencius on Motivation to Be Moral," published in *Philosophy East and West* 60(1) (2010): 65–87; Chapter 4 uses material from my "Can Virtue Be Taught and How?: Confucius on the Paradox of Moral Education," published in *Journal of Moral Education* 40(2) (2011): 141–59. I would like to thank their original publishers for their permissions. I read a paper drawn from materials in Chapter 2 at a conference at Sungkyungkwan University in Seoul and Nishan Forum in Qufu, China and a paper drawn from materials in Chapter 5 at a conference at Huafan University in Taipei, both in May 2012. I would like to thank Professor Tae-Seung Lim of Sungkyungkwan and Professor Jen-Kuen Chen of Huafan Univeristy for their invitation and Professor Myeong-seok Kim of Sungkyungkwan University for his comments on the paper presented there.

I would like to thank Mrs. Laurel Delaney, who read the whole manuscript, as she did with almost every other publication of mine, helping me improve my expressions and avoid many infelicities, Mr. Mark McClenithan, who helped in creating a list of the entries for the index, and Professor John Lizza, the chair of the Philosophy Department of Kutztown University, who has supported my research throughout the years in various ways.

I also would like to thank Kirsty Schaper, the commissioning editor of Bloomsbury, for inviting me to write this book, Rachel Eisenhauer, the editorial assistant of Bloomsbury, for her admirable professionalism when I was procrastinating with this project, Joanne Murphy, the production manager of the book, for overseeing the publication process, and Srikanth Srinivasan, for his efficient copyediting, typesetting, and proofreading.

CHAPTER ONE

The life of Confucius: "A homeless dog?"

1. Introduction

Confucianism is clearly related to the person Confucius, which is the Latinized form of Kong Fuzi 孔夫子 (551–479 BCE), who lived in ancient China during the Spring and Autumn period (722–481 BCE), part of the East Zhou 周 Dynasty (770–256 BCE). Kong is the family name, while Fuzi is an honorific name, meaning master. His given name is Qiu 丘, literally meaning mountain. As his parents prayed for him at the mountain of Ni when his mother was pregnant with him, his official name is Zhongni, where Zhong is a middle name indicating the seniority in his family as the second son and Ni refers to the name of the mountain. Most frequently, however, he has been simply addressed as Kongzi, where *zi* means something similar to *fuzi*, and so Kongzi means Master Kong.

"A homeless dog" was one of the many descriptions a stranger gave of Confucius when he was traveling across different states, selling his vision of government, with no avail, and was the only one that Confucius accepted. While it is particularly true of him during that period of wandering, it is also quite adequate as a description of his whole life. Even during the heydays of his political career in his home state of Lu, he was not able to fully implement his political ideas. In this sense, Confucius's political life, which he cherished greatly, was a failure. However, as a moral educator, he has been remembered and has exerted great influence throughout Chinese history and beyond.

2. Shining ancestry and humble childhood

Referring to his ancestors, Confucius said that he was a person of Yin 殷 (*Liji* 3.49). As a matter of fact, he was from the royal family of Yin, the ruling ethnic group in the later part of the second dynasty of China, Shang 商 (1600–1043 BCE). This part of the Shang dynasty is also called Yin dynasty, starting from 1298 BCE, when the tenth emperor Pan'geng 盘庚 moved its capital from Yan 奄 to Yin 殷, in present Anyang 安陽 of Henan province, until the dynasty was conquered by King Wu 武 of Zhou and replaced by the Zhou 周 Dynasty (1046–770 BCE for West Zhou and 770–256 BCE for East Zhou). After conquering Yin, in order to comfort the Yin people, King Wu of Zhou enfeoffed Wugeng 武庚, the son of the last emperor of Yin/Shang dynasty, Zhou 紂, as the duke in the area native to the Yin people (part of the present Henan province). Wugeng rebelled when King Wu of Zhou died, but this rebellion was suppressed by King Wu's brother, Duke Dan of Zhou. Acting as a regent while the son of King Wu, King Cheng, was still young, Duke Dan of Zhou divided the Yin people's native place into three parts, of which the eastern part was established as the state of Song 宋. Still to comfort the Yin people, Weizi 微子, the brother of Zhou 紂, who surrendered in the rebellion, was enfeoffed as the duke of the state of Song.

After Weizi died, his younger brother Weizhong 微仲, the direct ancestor of Confucius, succeeded as the duke. Between Weizhong and Confucius, there were 15 generations, of which the following are worth mentioning. Four generations after Weizhong was Duke Min 緡, who had two sons, Fufuhe 弗父何 and Fushi 鮒祀. When Min died, he designated his brother, Yang 煬, to succeed him as duke. As the custom prevalent at the time was to let a son succeed his father, Fushi killed his uncle Yang and tried to make his own brother Fufuhe the Duke, which Fufuhe declined, thinking that he would then have to punish his brother for the crime of killing the duke, their uncle. Thus Fushi himself became the king, while Fufuhe, the eleventh generation ancestor of Confucius, became a hereditary minister (*qin* 卿) and was remembered for having the virtue of deference for not taking the dukeship. To that point, the status of Confucius's ancestors gradually declined first from the Royal family of the Yin dynasty to the duke of Song state and from that to a hereditary minister.

Fufuhe's third generation grandson Zhengkaofu 正考父 successively served three dukes and was remembered for his diligence. His son, Confucius's sixth generation grandfather, Kongfujia 孔父嘉, was killed in a court coup. His son Mujinfu 木金父 fled to the state of Lu 鲁 and began using Kong as the family name. He resided in Zou 鄹, southeast of the present Qufu 曲阜 of Shangdong Province. Without the dukedom, the Kong family no longer belonged to the noble class, but they were not commoners either. Instead, they belonged to *shi* 士, a class between the nobles and common people (sometimes regarded as the lowest stratum of nobles or the highest stratum of common people), whose job was to serve hereditary ministers with their knowledge and/or skills. The first two generations of the Kong family did not attract the attention of rulers in their new home state, Lu. The third generation, Kong Fangshu 孔防叔, assumed a position of the lower level official under a noble family, while his grandson Shulianghe 叔梁纥, Confucius's father, was the head of the small town of Zou 鄹, an official position in the state of Lu. For this reason, he is sometimes also called Zou Lianghe or Zou Shuhe, and Confucius called himself the son of the Zou people (*Analects* 3.15). Shulianghe was known for his bravery and extraordinary strength, particularly in two victorious battles where he heroically defended the state of Lu against attacks from the states of Jin 晋 (563 BCE) and Qi 齐 (556 BCE) respectively.

Shulianghe had nine daughters through his first marriage and a son with a lame leg through a concubine. Eager to have a physically normal son to succeed him, Shulianghe asked to marry one of the daughters of the Yan family. The youngest daughter, Yan Zhengzai 顏征在, agreed and became Confucius's mother. Confucius was born on September 28, 551 BCE, as a result of the *yehe* 野合, literally "wild union," between Shulianghe and Yan Zhengzai, according to the *Records of History* (*Shiji* 史記). There are scholarly disagreements about what *yehe* really means. According to one interpretation, since there was a gap of more than 40 years between Shulianghe (now over 60 years old) and Yan Zhengzai (less than 20 years old), the marriage between the two was against ritual propriety, and so it was *yehe* (see Kuang 1990: 22). According to another interpretation, this simply means that they were united in the wild and not inside a house.

According to another interpretation, this indicates that the birth of Confucius, a sage, is a resonance from heaven (Qian 2005: 4). According to yet another interpretation, this means that the two married without a matchmaker and appropriate rituals (Zhang 1997: 9); according to yet another interpretation, it means that Shulianghe raped Yan Zhengzai (Cai 1982: 5). In any case, because his parents prayed for a son at Mount Ni, Confucius was also named Kong Qiu, where *qiu* literally means "mountain," and Zhongni, where *"ni"* is after the name of mountain, while *"zhong"* is the term used to indicate that he was the second son (his stepbrother Boni 伯尼 was the first). Confucius is also called, often derogatorily, especially in China's anti-Confucius campaigns in the 70s of last century, KONG Lao'er 孔老二, literally Kong The Number 2.

When Confucius was only 3 years old, his father died, and his mother left the Kong family and carried Confucius to Qufu, the then capital of the state of Lu, where many of the Yan clan members lived. Although they got some help from these relatives, since most of them were commoners, their life was hard, and Confucius had many chores to do to support the family. Confucius's mother died, perhaps from excessive labor, when she was less than 40 years old. From then on, Confucius was entirely on his own. When he married Qiguan Shi 亓官氏 at the age of 19 and had his only son, Kong Li 孔鲤, a year later, Confucius had to work even harder to take care of his family. When he was in his 20s, he worked for noble families, once taking care of horses and sheep and once doing the bookkeeping. In each case, Confucius did an impressive job (see *Mencius* 5b5). Thus Confucius later recalled: "I was in a humble station when I was young, and that is why I am skilled in many menial things" (*Analects* 9.6), although he said that a superior person does not have to learn such things.

Even when enduring hardship, Confucius's mother didn't neglect his education. It is believed that an additional reason that they moved to the state of Lu after the death of Confucius's father was that, as the home state of Duke of Zhou, Lu was rich in cultural tradition. While unable to go to official schools for noble classes, Confucius was sent to schools for commoners, which were open only off the harvest seasons. Confucius said that "I set my mind on learning when I was fifteen" (*Analects* 2.4), without a fixed teacher. Thus, when asked about the teacher from whom Confucius acquired his learning, Zigong, one of his students, replied, "where doesn't my teacher learn? Why have there to be a fixed teacher?" (*Analects* 19.22).

The content of his learning includes everything necessary for a member of the *shi* class, particularly the so-called six arts. First, even when he was very young, he was interested in rituals so much that, while his childhood friends played with their toys, he practiced ritual performance with simple ritual utensils for fun at home (see Sima 2008). When he was a little older, he studied rituals by reading ancient books, including the *Book of Poetry* and the *Book of Documents*. By the time his mother died, when he was only 17 years old, he was able to handle the burial properly. According to rituals, his mother was to be buried at the same place as his father. However, he was only 3 when his father died, and his mother never told him where he was buried. So in consistence with ritual propriety, he temporarily buried his mother at a public land until he learned the location of his father's graveyard from one of his neighbors. Then he buried his mother permanently at the same place. In order to learn about the rituals of the Yin dynasty, he made a special trip to the State of Song, the native place of the Yin people. When he was 27, Tanzi, the ruler of the small state of Tan 郯, visited the state of Lu. After learning that Tanzi was a very erudite person, Confucius asked to meet him to learn about the titles and other things related to state officials. On one occasion, Confucius had a chance to get into the state temple in Lu, a place for making sacrifice to Duke of Zhou. He asked questions about almost every ritual performed there. When he was laughed at for both being ritually inappropriate in asking questions while people were performing rituals and for his fake reputation as a person versed in rituals, Confucius made a three-word response (*Analects* 3.15), which has been subject to two different interpretations. According to one interpretation, Confucius's reply was: "this is ritually appropriate," meaning that it is ritually appropriate to ask people whenever you don't know something (Yang 1980: 28). According to another interpretation, Confucius's reply was: "is that ritually appropriate?" meaning that what was performed in the temple was not ritually appropriate, and Confucius kept asking questions in order to force people to reflect on what they were performing so that they could realize their mistakes (see Qian 2005: 69).

Second, there is a story about Confucius's study of music from Shi Xiangzi 師襄子, the state musician of Lu. Once he played one piece of music for ten days, and Shi Xiangzi suggested that he could play a different piece as he was familiar with old one. Confucius replied that, "while I'm familiar with the piece, I have not grasped its techniques." After a few days, Shi Xiangzi suggested that he could play a different piece as he now had grasped its technique. Confucius replied that, "while I have grasped its technique, I have not understood its meaning." After a few more days, Shi Xiangzi suggested that he play a different piece as he had now understood its meaning. Confucius replied that, "while I have understood its meaning, I have not figured out the personality of the composer yet." After still a few days, Confucius said, "Now I know the composer: he has dark skin, is very tall, and looks upward, and has the country unified. Who can that be other than King Wen?" Shi Xiangzi was very surprised, saying that his teacher had indeed told him that King Wen was the composer (see Sima 2008). Confucius enjoyed music so much that, later, on a trip to the State of Qi to discuss and perform music with royal musicians, he forgot the taste of meat for three months (*Analects* 7.14). He was even believed to be able to tell the difference between two sage kings' music: Shun's *shao* music is fully good and fully beautiful, while King Wu's *wu* music is fully beautiful and not fully good.

While we don't have particular information about how he learned the other four arts, it is clear that he must have learned them when he was young. When hearing people saying that he knows many things but is not proficient in any of them, Confucius said to his students: "What am I proficient at? Charioteering? Charioteering? Yes, I'm proficient in charioteering" (*Analects* 9.2). This shows that he must have learned to charioteer when he was young. Similarly, we learn that once, when Confucius was practicing archery, he was surrounded by a large crowd of spectators, which indicates that Confucius must have had astonishing archery skill (*Liji* 46.7; 836). The fact that he did an impressive job as a bookkeeper for a noble family when he was a little over 20 years old also shows that he must have been good at mathematics, while writing must be something he had already learned at the unofficial school he attended when he was very young.

3. Confucius establishes himself

Late in his life, Confucius looked back at the main stages of his life. After the first stage, when he was 15, at which he set his heart–mind on learning, Confucius said that he established himself when he was 30 years old as the second major landmark of his life (*Analects* 2.4). What he meant is that he knew how to say and do the right thing in any situation. Believing that "one who wants to establish oneself ought to establish others" (*Analects* 6.30), Confucius was among the earliest to open schools outside the governmental system to help others establish themselves. The official schools accepted only children of noble families. Confucius, however, made it clear that he taught people without discrimination (*Analects* 15.39). As a matter of fact, most of his students, such as Zilu 子路, Qidiao Kai 漆雕開, Minzi Qian 閔子騫, Yan Wuyou 顏無繇 (the father of Confucius's most favorite student Yan Hui 顏回), and Zeng Xi 曾皙 (the father of Confucius's student Zeng Sen 曾參, most famous for his virtue of filial piety), were all from the lower classes. This is of course understandable, as the children of noble families had official schools to go to, while people of the lower classes did not. However, the difference between Confucius's school and the official schools was not only about the type of students they had but also about the educational content. The traditional official schools primarily taught the so-called six arts, rituals, music, writing, mathematics, archery, and charioteering. Although Confucius himself was skilled at all of them, his teaching focused on classics, such as the *Book of Poetry*, the *Book of Document*, the *Book of Rites*, and the *Book of Music*. In other words, Confucius's teaching was primarily not the practical skills but the virtuous characters necessary not only for officials but also for all human beings.

Confucius's school soon established its reputation, and some noble families began to send their children to him. For example, Mengxizi 孟僖子, a high level official in the state of Lu, who was once embarrassed in a diplomatic trip to the state of Chu for not being familiar with rituals, sent his two children, Mengyizi 孟懿子 and Nan'gong Jingshu 南宮敬叔, to study with Confucius, and so they were also among Confucius's earliest students. As a student of Confucius, in 518 BCE, Nan'gong Jingshu asked Duke Zhao of

Lu for permission to take a trip with Confucius to Luoyi 洛邑 (the present day Luoyang of He'nan province), the then capital city of the Zhou Dynasty. In addition to examining the rituals, cultural relics, and classics, their main purpose was to visit the Daoist Laozi, who was then the minister of documents (compatible to the present day curator of the national museum or library) of the Zhou dynasty. Much older than Confucius, Laozi also knew much more about things that Confucius wanted to know most, rituals. Particularly, Confucius learned from Laozi what to do when there is an eclipse on the way to funeral proceedings; whether a child, when dying young, should be buried near or far; in what situation it is right to go to war when one is still in a mourning period for one's parent; and how to handle the funeral of an emperor or a king, etc. This meant a great deal for Confucius, as he later often mentioned these to his students. However, even more important was perhaps what Laozi said when Confucius came to say good bye: "to see their visitors off, rich people give valuable things, while wise people give advice. Since I'm not rich, let me pretend to be a wise person," and the following is the advice he gave to Confucius: "People good at business tend to hide their wealth as if they didn't have anything. People rich in virtues look like fools. You should get rid of arrogance, insatiability, assertiveness, and illusions" (Sima 2008a). Clearly, Confucius took what Laozi said to his heart, as he still praised Laozi to his students after he returned to Lu: "I know birds can fly, but they may be shot by people; I know fish can swim, but they may be caught by people; I know beasts can run, but they may be trapped by people. There is only one thing that we cannot control. It may come through clouds if it wants to, and it may leave through winds if it wants to. It may go to heaven if it wants to. This is the legendary dragon. I cannot fully understand Laozi, but he is just like a dragon" (Sima 2008a).

After he returned to the State of Lu, Confucius witnessed the power struggle between Duke Zhao of Lu and his ministers, ending with Zhao's exile in the states of Qi and Jin and his eventual death in Jin 7 years later. Unable to bear to see rituals being distorted and music being twisted in such a way, and with no hope of seeing his political ideals realized in his home state, Confucius decided to go to the state of Qi with some of his students in 517 BCE, when he was 35 years old. Although Confucius had already established his reputation and met Duke Jin of Qi when the latter visited the state of Lu, in order to be able to see the duke Confucius took a position at the family of Gao Zhaozi 高昭子, a member of the Duke's inner circles. With Gao's introduction, Confucius was able to see Duke Jin, who asked for Confucius's advice on running a government. Thus Confucius said: "Ruler ought to act like a ruler, minister ought to act like a minister, father ought to act like a father, and son ought to act like a son." Without realizing that Confucius was referring to him as a ruler who didn't act like one and thinking instead that Confucius only meant to say that his ministers didn't act like ministers, Duke Jin entirely agreed with Confucius, saying that, if not acting as Confucius said, "even if we have a lot of grain, we will have nothing to eat" (*Analects* 12.11). A few days later, Duke Jin asked Confucius what the most important thing in governing a state was. Realizing that the duke lived an indulgent life, Confucius said it was to be frugal. Again thinking that it was directed to others, Duke Jin was very pleased with Confucius and considered asking Confucius to stay and serve in his government. This was never realized, due to strong opposition from his minister Yanzi 晏子, who convinced the duke that Confucius's ideals, particularly those about rituals, were too idealistic to be realized. After a few years, seeing no hope of practicing his political ideals, Confucius and his students returned to his home state of Lu.

Confucius resumed his teaching, accepting a group of new students, including Zigong 子貢 and Yan Hui 顏回. While rituals were still an important topic of his teaching, *ren* 仁, the virtue of humanity, became the most prominent theme in his conversations with his students. As his main goal was to prepare his students to be virtuous officials, he also discussed politics, both of his home state and of other states. Confucius was still interested in putting his own political ideals into practice, but he would not accept any official position unless he thought it was appropriate.

4. The height of Confucius's political career

After the death of Duke Zhao of Lu, the state was in the control of the Ji 季 family. Instead of letting one of Duke Zhao's sons succeed, the Ji family decided to let his brother become the feudal lord of the state, and it was Duke Ding 定 of Lu. However, ironically, not only did feudal lords of different states become more powerful than the emperor of the Zhou dynasty, and the hereditary ministers of these feudal lords became more powerful than the lords in many states (as Ji and other two families were more powerful than the duke of Lu), but even officials under these ministers became more powerful than the ministers themselves in some families. This was particularly the case with Yanghu 阳虎 of the Ji family. Thus Confucius deplored: "nowadays officials under ministers are controlling the destiny of the empire!" (*Analects* 16.2).

In 505 BCE, when Confucius was 47 years old, Yanghu, in order to further strengthen his own power and weaken the power of the other two hereditary families, invited Confucius to help him. As Confucius refused to see him, Yanghu had a cooked young pig sent to him as a present while he was away, thinking that Confucius would then have to come to see him, as according to custom, if a member of the *shi* ± class was not at home when an official of a noble family sent him a present, the former was supposed to go to the latter's house to thank him in person. To avoid seeing Yanghu and yet not dishonor the custom, Confucius went to thank Yanghu when he knew that Yanghu was not at home. However, Confucius still came across Yanghu unexpectedly on his way back. Yanghu said to him: "Can a man be regarded as humane if he has good ideas and yet let his state go astray? Of course not! Can a man be regarded as wise if he is eager to be an official but constantly misses opportunities? Of course not! Time goes by quickly and does not wait for us" (*Analects* 17.1). Confucius was somewhat moved and inclined to take the position, although he eventually did not. Instead, he began to edit classical texts such as the *Book of Poetry*, the *Book of Documents*, the *Book of Rituals*, and the *Book of Music*, to be used in his teaching.

Soon after his encounter with Yanghu, there was a conversation between Zigong, one of Confucius's students, and Confucius. Zigong asked, "If I have a beautiful jade, should I hide it in a drawer or sell it to a business person who appreciates it?" Confucius responded: "Sell it! Sell it! I'm waiting for a business person who appreciates it" (*Analects* 9.13). The time for him to sell his treasures finally came in 501 BCE, when he was 51 years old. Yanghu had fled the state of Lu after his failed coup in the same year. The state of Lu was now back in the control of the Ji family, with Ji

Huanzi 季桓子 serving as the chief minister to Duke Ding of Lu. With the lingering fear of the danger of "officers under ministers controlling the state," they started looking for people other than power-thirsty officials in the families of the three hereditary ministers, people with political ideals and moral integrity. Naturally they turned their attention to Confucius, who had acquired an increasing reputation for precisely what they wanted. However, the first job that Confucius had was relatively obscure: the head of Zhongdu 中都, a very small town. Perhaps the chief minister Ji and Duke Ding were assigning Confucius a trial appointment. In this position, Confucius governed the town with rituals, focusing on the moral cultivation of its people, with great success. Within a year, people were taken care of when living and properly buried when dead, old people and young people ate different foods, strong and weak people did different jobs, men and women walked on different sides of the road, no one would pick up and pocket things others lost on the road, and no one sold forgeries. These practices soon spread to neighboring towns. Duke Ding of Lu was very pleased, asking Confucius, "what do you think about using the measures you used here to govern the state of Lu?" Confucius said, without any modesty, "they can even be used to govern the whole empire of Zhou, let alone the state of Lu" (*Kongzi Jiayu* 1; 1).

So in the second year, Confucius was promoted to the position of assistant minister of public works at the state level. Although he served in this position for only a brief period of time, he accomplished at least two noteworthy things. First, he analyzed the state's landholdings and classified them into five different types, suitable to different types of plants. Second, he changed the arrangement of the tombs of the deceased dukes. After Duke Zhao of Lu died in exile, in order to degrade him, his body was taken back to the state of Lu but was buried south of the tombs of the previous dukes, separated by a road. This was done by the then chief minister Ji Pingzi 季平子, father of the current chief minister Ji Huanzi, whom now Confucius was serving. Confucius persuaded Ji Huanzi that this ritual impropriety, which degraded Duke Zhao, actually gave his father, Ji Pingzi, a bad reputation. It could be cleared, however, by rearranging the tombs. Confucius thus dug a ditch south of the tomb of Duke Zhao, which now joined the tombs of all other deceased dukes of Lu, as they were all to the north of the ditch.

In less than a year, Confucius was promoted to the minister of justice, one of the three most important positions under the duke in the state of Lu. This was the high point in Confucius's political career. He was then 52 years old. As the minister of justice, Confucius's main job was to judge cases. Before a decision was made, Confucius tended to ask those who were familiar with or had opinions on the case for their opinions. After this, Confucius would decide whose opinion was right and then make the appropriate decision. However, Confucius confessed that in terms of judging cases, he was not any better than other people; what made him different from others was his attempt to do all that he could so that the legal case would not arise in the first place (*Analects* 12.13).

As the minister of justice, Confucius had more opportunities to meet Duke Ding of Lu, to whom he provided political advice on a number of occasions. The *Analects* records two of them. On one occasion, Duke Ding asked Confucius how a ruler should use his ministers and how ministers should serve their ruler. Confucius replied, "the ruler should use his ministers according to rules of propriety, and ministers should serve their ruler by doing their best" (*Analects* 3.19). On another occasion, Duke Ding asked Confucius, "Is there such a thing as one saying causing the prosperity of a state?" Confucius replied, "one saying cannot quite do that. However, here is the saying: 'it is difficult to be a ruler, and it is not easy to be a minister.' Now if a ruler knows the difficulty of being a ruler [he would naturally do his best], then this saying would almost cause the prosperity of the state." Duke Ding further asked, "Is there such a thing as one saying causing the destruction of a state?" Confucius replied, "one saying cannot quite do that. However, here is a saying, 'The only joy I have for being a ruler is that whatever I say, no one would go against it.' Now if what is said is correct, of course it is good. Yet if what is said is not correct, and no one is against it, then it is close to destroying the state" (*Analects* 13.15).

The brightest single event for Confucius during his tenure as the minister of justice, perhaps even in his whole life, was no doubt his handling as the minister of rituals on the occasion of the summit between Duke Ding of Lu with Duke Jing 景 of Qi in an open place called Jiagu 夹谷 in 500 BCE. The state of Qi at that time was much stronger than Lu. However, Qi was at war with another strong state, Jin 晉, with which Lu was an ally. Qi wanted Lu to be on its side, while Lu also intended to switch sides as Qi became stronger than Jin. The meeting between the heads of these two states was intended to negotiate a treaty. Thinking that Confucius was a person familiar only with rituals but not military matters, Duke Jin of Qi, persuaded by his ministers, decided to use the armed people of Lai, a local non-Chinese ethnic group conquered by and subjected to the state of Qi, to force Duke Ding of Lu to make concessions. Having anticipated that, Confucius persuaded his boss to have adequate military people and equipment accompany them, saying that diplomatic activities should always be accompanied by military power, just as military activities should always be accompanied by diplomatic maneuvers. Still, he protected his boss and defended the interests of his state largely through his knowledge of ritual propriety.

In the middle of the meeting, the armed Lai people came to the stage, pretending to dance, and threatened Duke Ding of Lu. Confucius stood out, requesting Duke Jin of Qi to send out his military to drive out the Lai people, saying: "Our two rulers are here having a friendly meeting, and to allow barbarian prisoners of war to do violence here is certainly not the way your Majesty treats dukes of Chinese states. People from distant borders are not allowed to make trouble to people at the central plain, barbarians are not allowed to separate Chinese people, prisoners of war are not allowed to interfere with our alliance, and force cannot produce friendship. Such actions are not respectful to our spirit, are destructive of our moral principle, and are ritually inappropriate to human beings. Your Majesty would certainly not allow this to happen!" (*Zuozhuan*: Duke of Ding, Year 10). Finding no faults in what Confucius said, Duke Jin of Qi ordered the Lai people to leave, and a treaty, on terms better to the state of Lu than Duke Ding even expected, was signed between the two states without military interference. After the treaty was signed, the state of Qi proposed a banquet. Afraid of having further complications, Confucius refused, saying that "to take dining utensils suitable for the heads of our two states to such a wild place was against ritual propriety, and allowing the heads of our states to use dinner utensils for people of lower stations was also against ritual propriety." Returning home, Duke Jin of Qi complained to his ministers thus: "Confucius assisted his ruler with ritual propriety, while you asked me to do the wrong thing by using the violence of barbarian people" (Sima 2008).

After this diplomatic victory, Confucius's reputation rose rapidly, and he won further trust and praise from both Duke Ding and Ji Huanzi, the chief minister who held the actual power of the state. At age 54 and through Ji Huanzi's arrangement, in 498 BCE, Confucius was appointed acting chief minister, handling the most important matters on behalf of Ji Huanzi, and thus became the third most important figure in the state of Lu. This was the best time for Confucius to practice his political ideal, which was essentially to strengthen the central power of the emperor of the Zhou dynasty and support the local lords of different states, while suppressing the power of the hereditary ministers of the state and weakening the power of officials within the houses of these hereditary ministers.

Confucius believed that, "when the Way prevails in the empire, rites, music, and punitive expeditions come from the emperor; When the Way disappears from the empire, rites, music, and punitive expeditions come from the local lords. If they come from the local lords, then power can hardly last ten generations; if they come from hereditary ministers, the power can hardly last five generations; if they come from the officials within the houses of these hereditary ministers, then the power can hardly last three generations" (*Analects* 16.2). The actual situation of the state of Lu at this time was precisely the last case: not only was its feudal lord, Duke Ding, all but nominal, without actual power, with the state being controlled by ministers from the three hereditary families; but even within the houses of these three families, the ministers were controlled by their own appointed officials.

This was something that Confucius wanted to change. He devised a plan to destroy the three capitals, which were originally three houses built in three small towns, all close to the border, that the duke of the state gave to the three hereditary families. Throughout the years, as the power of these three families gradually increased, each of the three houses expanded into a capital, controlled by officials appointed by the three families, as the three hereditary ministers were all living in Qufu 曲阜, the capital city of the State of Lu. Duke Ding of Lu liked the idea, and it was also approved by Ji Huanzi, even though one of the three capitals to be destroyed was his. He himself suffered from the overreaching power of officials controlling his capital in his own house. One of the three capitals, that of the Shusun 叔孫 family, was easily destroyed. When it was time to destroy Ji Huanzi's capital, Confucius encountered strong resistance from its officials but was able to conquer it eventually. However, although the minister of the third capital, Mengsun 孟孫, originally accepted Confucius's plan, the officials who controlled his capital had always been loyal to him. Realizing that he would not benefit from destroying his own capital, he secretly supported his officials in resisting. The capital was not destroyed, even after extended fighting, by forces led by Duke Ding himself. At the same time, the other two ministers whose capitals had been destroyed started to realize that, while they originally supported Confucius's plan in order to weaken the power of officials controlling their capitals, Confucius's purpose was additionally to weaken the power of the three hereditary ministers themselves in order to strengthen the power of the Duke of Lu. They thus no longer sided with Confucius. Since the actual power of the state of Lu was not controlled by Duke Ding but by these three ministers, particularly Ji Huanzi, there were only two roads left for Confucius, either to drop his political ideal of strengthening the public power of the state and even of the empire and serve the interests of these three hereditary families, particularly that of Ji Huanzi, or to leave his position. Confucius chose the latter and started his 14 years of travel, followed by a group of his students, from one state to another, looking for a ruler who truly appreciated his political ideas.

5. "A homeless dog" on the way

It was 497 BCE, and Confucius was 55 years old. We may divide these 14 years into three main periods.

5.1 In the State of Wei (497 BCE–493 BCE)

The first state Confucius went to was not Qi to the east of Lu but Wei 衛 to the west. He was sure that Qi had not forgotten what he did at the summit meeting between Qi and Lu in the place of Jiagu. Several things drew him to Wei. First, "in terms of government, the states of Lu and Wei are like brothers" (*Analects* 13.7). Second, Qi had a worthy minister, Ju Boyu 蘧伯玉. Confucius respected him, and he had sent a visitor to see Confucius a few years earlier. In the *Analects*, there is the following record: Confucius asked the person sent by Ju Boyu: "what is your master doing?" and the messenger replied, "he is trying to reduce errors but has not succeeded." After the messenger left, Confucius said to his students: "this is a good messenger; this is a good messenger" (*Analects* 14.26). Confucius spoke of Ju Boyu very highly, "What a superior person Ju Boyu is! When the Way prevails in the state, he took office; and when the Way falls into disuse, he put away his governing skills safely" (*Analects* 15.5). Third, there were personal connections. While several students of Confucius were originally from the state of Wei, one of Duke Ling of Wei's favorite ministers, Mizi 弥子, was the brother-in-law of Confucius's student Zilu, whose wife was the sister of Mizi's wife.

On their way, seeing a flourishing population in Wei, Ranyou 冉有, one of Confucius's students, asked, "to the flourishing population, what can be added?" Confucius replied, "to make them rich." Ranyou further asked, "to a rich population, what can be added?" and Confucius replied, "to educate them" (*Analects* 13.9). After their arrival in Wei, with Mizi's introduction, Duke Ling of Wei soon received Confucius. Given Confucius's high reputation, Duke Ling paid Confucius the same salary as he was paid when he served the state of Lu, which was more than enough to support Confucius and a group of his students. However, he did not give Confucius any actual position. He wanted Confucius primarily to promote his own image. As a matter of fact, the duke was at that time busy preparing an attack on the state of Jin, while Confucius was interested in governing a state with rituals and virtues.

According to a record in the *Analects*, one day, "Duke Ling of Wei sought Confucius's advice on military matters. Confucius replied, 'I've learned something about the use of ritual utensils, but I have never learned anything on military matters.' The second day Confucius left the state of Wei" (*Analects* 15.1). There was another reason why Confucius decided to leave. Once when Duke Ling of Wei and Confucius were having a conversation, a bird suddenly appeared flying above them. The duke looked at the bird for a long time without listening to what Confucius said, which for Confucius was not only against ritual propriety but also indicated that the duke was not really interested in what he had to say about government. However, perhaps the most important reason was neither of these. There was a worthy man, Gongshu Wenzi 公叔文子, a deceased senior minister in Wei, whom Confucius spoke of very highly. After he arrived in Wei, Confucius also asked people about Gongshu Wenzi's deeds and words (see *Analects* 14.13 and 14.18). Moreover, Gongshu's son, Gongshu Xu 公叔戍, now succeeding in his father's position, asked Confucius's students about funeral rituals. However, Gongshu Xu, unlike his father, was arrogant and initiated a failed coup. Someone told Duke Ling of Wei that Confucius was possibly involved with this coup, given their close relationship. So the duke had someone follow Confucius wherever he went. This was of course not something Confucius could bear.

After just 10 months, Confucius and his students decided to leave Wei. When they left, among his followers, in addition to those who came with him from Lu, there was a new student, Gongliang Ru 公良孺, from a noble family in the state of Chen 陳, who added five horse-drawn carriages to the group. This time Confucius decided to go to the state of Chen. However, two unexpected events took place, which aborted his plan. The first occurred when they passed through a small town called Kuang 匡, a place attacked 7 years earlier by troops of the state of Lu commanded by Yanghu 阳虎, who killed many Kuang people. The person who drove Confucius's carriage had participated in that attack. While telling people about that attack, he was heard by some Kuang people at the roadside, and they mistook Confucius, sitting in the carriage and followed by a large group of people, for Yanghu, as they looked somewhat alike.

Learning of this, the head of the town sent solders to arrest Confucius and his followers. Confucius was kept in an empty room, and his students all came to his side. Yan Hui, Confucius's most favorite student, came in last. Seeing him, Confucius was relieved, saying, "I was afraid that you were killed." And Yan Hui responded, "You, master, are still alive; how could I dare to die" (*Analects* 11.23). While in custody, some of Confucius's students suggested forcing a way out, and Confucius disagreed, saying, "with the death of King Wen, is not culture invested in me? If it were the intention of Heaven to destroy this culture, I would not have had any part of it. However, since Heaven does not intend to destroy it, what can Kuang people do to me?" (*Analects* 9.5). On the following day, the fifth day of their custody, they were eventually released as the Kuang people were convinced that Confucius was not Yanghu.

After their release, they planned to go to a place near the border of Wei to rest, but the second unexpected event took place when they passed through a place called Pu 蒲. Pu was enfeoffed to the Gongshu family. After his failed coup, Gongshu Xu fled to Pu to prepare his next rebellion against Duke Ling of Wei. When Confucius and his followers went to this place, they were stopped and asked to join the rebellion. Several students, particularly Zilu and newly joined Gongliang Ru, couldn't bear this, as they had just gotten free from the trouble in Kuang. So they led the fight against Gongshu Xu's people. At the end, realizing that it would not help them to keep Confucius and his students, Gongshu Xu allowed them to leave, under the condition that they would not return to Diqiu 帝丘, the capital of the state of Wei.

However, as soon as they left Pu, Confucius decided to return to Diqiu. His student Zigong was puzzled, "could you not keep the promise you just made?" and Confucius replied, "this was a promise made under force and would not be acknowledged by spirit" (Sima 2008). What Confucius did at Pu convinced Duke Ling of Wei that Confucius had nothing to do with Gongshu Xu's rebellion, and so he personally welcomed Confucius upon his return. He asked Confucius whether it was feasible to attack Pu, and Confucius replied yes. Duke told Confucius that his ministers didn't agree, thinking that Pu served as a barrier against invasion from the states of Chu and Jin. Confucius explained: the people of Pu were not willing to join Gongshu's rebellion and had the determination to defend their home state, Wei, against invasion. What the duke needed to do was to attack only four or five leaders there. Although the duke thought Confucius was right, he was still hesitant to initiate this attack; soon Gongshu Xu himself left Pu and fled to the state of Lu.

Confucius was again well treated with a big salary without any actual position, but he was looking for an opportunity to practice his political ideals in Wei. For this reason, he accepted an invitation to a meeting from Duke Ling's wife, Nanzi 南子, who said that all guests from different places who would like to see Duke Ling would come to see her also. Nanzi was young, beautiful, smart, and had a heavy influence upon the politics of the state, but she also had a bad reputation for being licentious in sexual conduct. As Confucius was very well-known, she wanted to see what kind of person he was. Knowing that he cared a lot about ritual propriety, Nanzi was well dressed, sitting behind the screen while talking to him, and did not say or do anything improper. However, Confucius's decision to see her was still not understood by his student Zilu, who was very unhappy about it, and so Confucius made a vow: "If I did anything improper, may Heaven's curse be on me! May Heaven's curse be on me!" (*Analects* 6.28). One of Duke Wei's ministers, Wang Sunjia 王孫賈, also did not want Confucius to visit Nanzi. He came to ask Confucius what the saying, "Better to flatter the kitchen stove than to the south-west corner of the house," means, with kitchen stove metaphorically referring to Wang himself and the south-west corner to Nanzi. Confucius replied, "Neither is right. If you have committed a crime against Heaven, it is of no use to pray to anyone" (*Analects* 3.13), showing that what he cared about was following the Way of Heaven.

In any case, this meeting appeared to be merely a matter of formality, and Confucius still didn't have anything to say about the politics in the state of Wei, although a number of his students were offered actual positions, the most important of which was Zilu's appointment as the head of the town of Pu after Gongshu Xu fled to the state of Lu. During this stay in Wei, anxious to practice his political ideals, Confucius attempted twice to leave Wei.

The first attempt was when an invitation came from Bixi 佛肸, the head of a town named Zhongmou 中牟, an enfeoffed land in the state of Jin. Bixi began a rebellion to make Zhongmou part of the state of Wei. While Confucius intended to go, his student Zilu was strongly against it, saying, "I previously heard from you, master, that a superior person does not enter a domain of the person who does what is not good himself. Now Bixi is using Zhongmou as a stronghold to rebel, and yet you decide to go. What is the reason?" Confucius replied, "Yes, I did say that. However, have you also heard it said that 'what is really hard can resist grinding, and what is truly white can withstand black dye?' Am I merely a gourd which hangs from the end of a string without allowing people to eat it?" (*Analects* 17.7). Even so, Confucius did not go, partly because of

Zilu's opposition and partly because of the complexity of the power struggle in the state of Jin.

The second attempt was his plan to see Zhao Yang 趙鞅, the chief minister of the state of Jin, as Jin was the most powerful state at the time, and so if his political ideals could be practiced there, the impact would be far greater than anywhere else. So in 494 BCE, Confucius, followed by Zigong and a few others, set off to go to Jin, which was on the west side of the Yellow River. However, even before they crossed the border of Wei, they heard that Zhao Yang killed two worthy ministers. Confucius was greatly disappointed and decided to quit the trip. Looking at the water flowing in the Yellow River, Confucius said, "I cannot go across the river. This is perhaps my fate!" (Sima 2008).

5.2 In the State of Chen (493 BCE–489 BCE)

Four years passed after Confucius first arrived in Wei. Although Duke Ling still treated him well, he did not seem to intend to give Confucius any substantial role to play in his government, wanting rather to use Confucius's reputation to promote his own image. This became clear in the following case. Duke Ling invited Confucius on a trip. He and his wife sat in the first carriage, while Confucius sat in the second one, blatantly seeking publicity. Not only did Confucius realize Duke Ling's intent to keep him in the state; he was also offended by the Duke's ritual impropriety of including his wife in this trip. About the latter, Confucius sighed: "I have not seen a person who loves virtues as he loves sex" (*Analects* 15.13).

In 493 BCE, when Confucius was 59 years old, he started to become anxious. Once, in such a mood, Confucius was playing the stone chimes. A passerby stopped, saying "the way you play the stone chimes carries a frustrated purpose": no one understood you. Then this passerby added, "if no one understood you, you must stop. If the water is deep, go across by wading; and if it is not that deep, then lift your hem and cross." Confucius understood what was meant: when society is very dark (water is deep), you can do nothing (go across without worrying about having your clothes getting wet); but when society is not so dark, try not to be polluted by it (lift your hem before crossing it); and so Confucius commented on what the passerby said, "how resolute it is, against which there is no argument" (*Analects* 14.39).

In that year, Duke Ling of Wei died. His heir apparent, his oldest son Kuaikui 蒯聵, unhappy with his stepmother Nanzi's deep involvement in Wei politics, had initiated a coup a few years earlier, and was exiled to the state of Jin. The crown was thus given to his son, Zhe 輒, who became Duke Chu 出. However, learning of his father's death, Kuaikui returned with his soldiers in an attempt to get the power back from his own son. Confucius's students wondered whether their master was on the side of Duke Chu of Wei, and so Zigong asked their master indirectly, "What kind of person were Boyi 伯夷 and Shuqi 叔齊?" Confucius replied, "they were worthy people in the ancient." Zigong further asked, "did they have complaints?" and Confucius replied, "they sought benevolence and got it. What complaints could they have?" Boyi and Shuqi were both princes, and they yielded to each other to take the crown by going abroad after their father died. This was in a clear contrast to Duke Chu and his father. So with this reply from Confucius, Zigong was sure that their master was not on Duke Chu's side (*Analects* 7.15).

As the atmosphere of the power struggle between the father and son led the state of Wei into chaos, Confucius finally decided to leave Wei. This time, he planned to go to the state of Chen 陳, as he had attempted to do previously. Between Wei and Chen, there were the states of Cao 曹 and Song 宋, among others. When they passed through Song, they were harassed by Huantui 桓魋, a high level official. Huantui was arrogant and selfish. He once ordered that a gigantic outer coffin be carved for him from a huge stone. This was an extremely demanding project. Workers toiled for 3 years, many becoming too weak and sick to continue, and it was still not finished. Learning of this, Confucius complained that, "instead of being so wasteful, I only wish Huantui's body decomposes quickly after he dies" (*Kongzi Jiayu* 42; 276). Huantui therefore did not care for Confucius. When he learned that Confucius and his students were in his own state, he decided to chase them out. One day, when Confucius and students were practicing rituals under a large tree, as they often did, near the place they stayed, Huantui sent people to chop the tree down and harass them. His students didn't want to see their teacher get hurt and suggested that they leave, but

Confucius said, "the Heaven gave birth to the virtue in me. What can Huantui do to me?" (*Analects* 7.23).

Even so, they decided to leave the state of Song for the state of Zheng 鄭. In order not to be recognized by people sent by Huantui, they changed into casual clothes and divided their large entourage into several small groups, which met at the city gate of Zheng's capital Xinzheng 新鄭. After a few days, students arrived at their destination before Confucius. Zigong was looking for Confucius, and a native of the city told him, "outside the east gate stands a person, very tall, with broad eyes and high forehead. His head looks like [sage King] Yao 尧, his neck looks like Gaoyao 皋陶 (Yao's minister of justice), his head looks like Zichan 子產, and from the waist down, he is three inches shorter than [sage king] Yu 禹. He is very tired, looking like a homeless dog." After Zigong told Confucius this native's descriptions of him, Confucius said, "I'm not sure whether I looked like these people as he described, but his description of me as a homeless dog is very accurate, very accurate" (*Kongzi Jiayu* 22; 153), clearly expressing his disappointment at not being able to persuade any ruler to adopt his political ideals.

Confucius and his students finally arrived in the state of Chen in 492 BCE, where he would stay for the next 3 years. They were treated well by Duke Min 湣 of Chen, who, having known Confucius as a person who stressed virtues and rituals, was also impressed by Confucius's broad knowledge in a number of striking cases. Soon after they arrived in Chen, an office building in the capital of Lu, Confucius's home state, caught a fire. Hearing this, Confucius said that perhaps this would burn down the neighboring temples for the two deceased Dukes of Lu, the eighth generation Duke Huan 桓 and the sixth generation Duke Xi 僖. Duke Min of Chen asked Confucius how he felt that way, and Confucius replied, "if the ancestors had virtues and great accomplishments, their temples should be preserved. However, the close relatives of Duke Huan and Duke Xi were all gone, and these two dukes didn't have enough virtues and accomplishments to have their temples kept. Since people of Lu have so far not destroyed them, now the heaven is going to do it." It turned out that his prediction was right. While not interested in what happened in the state of Lu, Duke Min of Chen was very impressed, saying, "now I know why sages deserve our respect" (*Kongzi Jiayu* 16; 116).

Another day, a bird fell from the sky down into the palace of Chen, shot by a wooden arrow with a stone head, very different from those used at the time. Curious about this type of arrow, Duke Min of Chen went to Confucius. Confucius told him that this was a very ancient arrow. After King Wu 武 of Zhou 周 conquered Shang 商, he asked each of the minority groups to contribute something unique, so that they would not forget their respective traditional occupations. One of these minority groups, Sushen 叔慎, made the king arrows. King Wu late gave these arrows to his daughter, who was married to Duke Hu 胡 of Chen. Confucius said that there were probably more such arrows, with the inscription "Arrows Contributed by Sushen," in the old warehouse of Chen. Duke Min was surprised when he indeed found them (*Guoyu:* Luyu 5.19; 220–1).

However, Duke Min of Chen, just like Duke Ling of Wei, wanted Confucius as a decoration, to show that he was a ruler who respected ritual propriety and virtue, yet had no intention of governing his state with virtues and ritual propriety as Confucius advised them to. Confucius was not appointed with any actual governmental position. With leisure time and in a peaceful environment, Confucius resumed his life-long vocation, for which he is remembered anyway, studying and teaching. During this period, in addition to those who continued to follow him, he accepted a few new students, most prominent among whom were Zizhang 子張, Zixia 子夏, and Ziyou 子游.

Unfortunately, this peaceful period did not last long. Chen was a small state, pulled by two large rival states, Chu 楚 and Wu 吳. Presently, Chen was allied with Chu. In 489 BCE, Wu attacked Chen, and Chu came to the rescue; thus a war between Wu and Chu was waged in the land of Chen. Clearly Chen was no longer suitable for Confucius and his students, and so they decided to leave. This time, their intended destination was the state of Chu. From Chen to Chu, they had to go through a place which was formerly the state of Cai 蔡, currently controlled by Wu. As there had just been a war, the place was largely deserted. The road was treacherous, and the trip was tiring and slow. After just a few days, their food ran out. Many became sick, and still more were so weakened by hunger that they could not stand. They decided to rest at an abandoned house. Given what they had experienced since leaving the state of Lu and what they were presently facing, the morale of the group was clearly low. It was Confucius who pulled everyone together.

One day, Zigong received some rice in exchange for his own clothes and other personal belongings. While Yan Hui was cooking, Zigong saw him take something and eat it. Zigong asked Confucius, "will a person of virtue and character become immoral when poor?" Confucius said, "how can an immoral person be regarded as one with virtue and integrity!" Zigong now asked more directly, "will not a person like Yan Hui become immoral?" "No!" Confucius said. After Zigong told Confucius what he had seen, Confucius called Yan Hui in and told him that the rice he cooked would be used to sacrifice to the ancestors. Yan Hui replied that the rice was not suitable for sacrifice, as some dust fell into the pot while he was cooking it. He thought that if he did nothing, the rice would be not clean, and it would be a waste if he threw it away. So he ate the part with dust. Confucius approved what Yan Hui did, saying that he would do the same if he were Yan Hui. Thus a misunderstanding was avoided (*Kongzi Jiayu* 20; 142–3).

Another day, coming back almost empty-handed from a search for food, Zigong and Zilu saw their master playing his music and singing. Zilu said angrily, "are there times when superior persons are so poor that they cannot do anything?" Confucius replied, "it is not unusual that superior persons, when poor, will still stand out, while inferior persons, when poor, will throw out all restraints" (*Analects* 15.2). Still, Confucius felt it necessary to know what his students were thinking. He asked his students: "Does the fact that we have to endure so many difficulties show that what I believe is not true?" Zilu was the first to say, bluntly: "perhaps you, my master, are not virtuous enough so that people don't believe you; or perhaps you, my master, are not wise enough, and so people don't want to adopt your ideas." Confucius responded: "do you really think that all virtuous people will be trusted? If so, why did Boyi 伯夷 and Shuqi 叔齊 starve to death on the Shouyang 首阳 Mountain? Do you really think that all wise people will necessarily be used? If so Prince Bigan 比干 would not be killed." Then he asked Zigong the same question, and Zigong responded: "Your teachings are too great and so no one under heaven can adopt it. Why don't you lower your standard a little bit?" Confucius said, "a superior person needs self-cultivation and establish a clear set of political principles, which are not necessarily acceptable by others. Zigong, if you don't cultivate yourself and only pay attention to being accepted by others, your aspiration is not great enough, and your thinking is not deep enough." Finally, he asked the same question of Yan Hui, his most favorite student, who responded, "master's teaching is greatest, and so it cannot be adopted. However, my master continues to promote it, and its not being accepted shows the ugliness of political rulers and has nothing to do with you. So the very fact that your teaching is not accepted shows that you are a superior person." Confucius was most pleased with Yan Hui's answer (*Kongzi Jiayu* 20; 139–40).

In any case, this was perhaps the most difficult period of time encountered during the entire 14 years of travel from one state to another. Finally, 7 days after their food ran out, they received help from the people of Fuhan 負函, another place which belonged to the State of Chu, and in which the Cai people lived. They soon arrived there. Confucius and his students were well received without any shortage of living necessities. The ruler of Fuhan, Shen Zhuliang 沈諸梁, was once the governor of a place nearby called She 叶, and so he was called Governor of She. He loved discussing politics with Confucius. Once, he asked how to govern, and Confucius replied: "to make people near happy and attract people far to come" (*Analects* 13.16). Another time he asked Zigong what kind of person his teacher was. Zigong didn't respond but he told Confucius. Confucius said, "why didn't you simply tell him that I am a person who tends to forget to eat when focusing on something and am full of joy, forgetting all worries, without noticing that the old age is coming?" (*Analects* 7.19). The following famous conversation between the governor and Confucius, which will become the main topic of Chapter Five of this book, also took place during this period. She told Confucius, "in our village there is an upright person named Zhigong. He bears evidence against his father stealing a sheep." And Confucius responded, "in my village, an upright person is different: father covers up son's wrongdoing, and son covers up father's wrongdoing, and the uprightness is in it" (*Analects* 13.18).

While in Fuhan, Confucius had a number of encounters with recluses. These were people who possessed knowledge and skills, but had given up hope. The *Analects* records a number of such encounters. The first was with the two recluses, Changju 長沮 and Jieni 桀溺, who were ploughing when Confucius sent Zilu to ask them where a ford was. Zilu first asked Changju, who responded by asking who the person in the carriage was. Zilu replied that it was Kong Qiu from the state of Lu. Changju then refused to answer, saying that Confucius must know where the ford was. Zilu then asked Jieni, who also asked about the person in the carriage. When Zilu told him, Jieni, knowing that he was a student of Kong Qiu, said, "bad things like flood are present everywhere under the heaven. With whom will you work to change it? Instead of following a person who keeps trying to escape bad people, why don't you follow those of us who escape the whole society?" Zilu told this to Confucius, who was disappointed, saying: "since we cannot associate ourselves with birds and beasts, with whom should we associate if not with human beings? If there is Way under heaven, I would not do any reform with you" (*Analects* 18.6).

On another occasion, Zilu, while traveling with Confucius, fell behind and asked an old man whether he saw his master. The man said, "You don't do any menial work and are unable to distinguish among five different kinds of grain. I don't know what kind of teacher you have." Then he invited Zilu to stay for the night and fed him chicken and millet. When Confucius commented that this must be another recluse, Zilu said, "it is not right to refrain from being governmental officials. The rules regulating the relationship between old and young cannot be set aside, and so how can the rightness between ruler and master be abandoned? If one tries to keep oneself from being sullied, one will cause confusion to the most important human relationships. Of course we know that the Way is not prevailing at this moment" (*Analects* 18.7).

On still another occasion, Jieyu 接輿, another recluse of Chu, went past Confucius's carriage, singing, "Phoenix, oh phoenix! Why are you so unlucky? What is past will not return, and what is to come is not yet lost. Give up! Give up! Perilous is the lot of those in office today." Confucius got out of the carriage to talk to him, but the recluse stepped up his pace to avoid him (*Analects* 18.5).

5.3 Back to the State of Wei (488 BCE–484 BCE)

In any case, Fuhan was not his destination. Confucius's original plan was to go to the capital of the state of Chu. However, before they set off, Confucius wanted to get in touch with the newly crowned Duke Hui 惠 of Chu and so sent his students Zixia 子夏 and Ranqiu

冉求 directly to the Chu capital Ying 郢 to learn about the situation there. King Zhao 昭 of Chu did want to use Confucius, but his chief minister was strongly opposed. After King Zhao died in 498 BCE, the possibility of being used by the Chu state was almost nonexistent. Moreover, although Confucius did not change his conviction about the importance of entering political life because of what the recluses said, the very existence of such recluses in the state of Chu, for Confucius, indicated that the government here was not using good people. Thus they decided not to proceed to Ying. At the same time, the situation in the state of Song was stabilized. Kuaikui was unable to overthrow Duke Chu, his own son, who consolidated his power. Those of his students who held official positions in the state of Song and so had not followed Confucius on this trip also sent a message, saying that Duke Chu intended to employ Confucius. So they decided to return to Song.

Learning that Duke Chu of Wei would give Confucius an important position, Zilu asked Confucius on their way back, "if the lord of Wei lets you govern the state, what would you do first?" Confucius replied, "it must be rectification of name." Zilu said, "Is that so? You are so pedantic! What is the need for rectification of the name?" Confucius replied: "How boorish you are! . . . When names are not correct, what is said will not sound logical; when what is said does not sound logical, then nothing will be accomplished; when nothing is accomplished, then rites and music will not flourish; when rites and music don't flourish, then punishment will not be made according to the crime; when punishment is not made according to the crime, then common people won't know where to put their hands and feet" (*Analects* 133). According to this idea of rectification of name, rulers should act like rulers, ministers should act like ministers, father should act like father, and son should act like son. This, however, is not something that sounded good to either side of the father–son power struggle in Wei: Kuaikui, supposedly a minister, was the father, while Duke Chu, the ruler, was a son.

So when they eventually returned to Wei, Duke Chu, just like his predecessor and grandfather, Duke Wei, gave Confucius a big salary but no significant position. Growing old, Confucius thought of returning to his home state Lu. At this time, the ruler of Lu was Duke Ai 哀, but Ji Kangzi 季康子, the son of Ji Huanzi, actually held power as the chief minister. Several of Confucius's students, such as Youruo 有若, Zigong 子貢, and Fan Chi 樊遲, had official positions and were doing impressive jobs. The state of Wu had an expansionist policy in those years, which threatened the state of Lu. In 488 BCE, Ji Kangzi asked Confucius's student Zigong to come along, who helped him not only avoid a humiliation but also score a diplomatic victory. In 487 BCE, Wu initiated a military attack on Lu. Confucius's student Youruo joined the resistance and forced the Wu force to withdraw. Given the dangerous situation of the state and the significant help he got from some of Confucius's students, Ji Kangzi first asked another of Confucius's students, Ranqiu 冉求, to return to Lu to be the head of his own hereditary house. At this Confucius was very happy, saying "Go home! Go home! Our young people back home have high aspirations with great accomplishments. I don't know how to teach them" (*Analects* 5.22). Soon after returning to the state of Lu, Ranqiu led a military force from Ji's house and won a brilliant victory against the invasion from the state of Qi. Ji Kangzi was very much impressed. He asked Ranqiu where he learned his military skills. "From my teacher Confucius" was the response. Ranqiu further told Ji Kangzi that Confucius was a person who, if employed, was certain to do wonderful things for people.

6. Return to home state

Ji Kangzi invited Confucius and his students to return to Lu. He sent three representatives, carrying with them a large present, to Wei to escort Confucius home. It was 484 BCE, 14 years since he had left Lu, and Confucius was now 68 years old. Confucius and his group were welcomed by those students of his who either did not accompany him during the 14 years or returned before him, as well as old friends and officials. Confucius was very moved by this. The only thing regrettable was that his wife had died a year earlier, while Confucius was still in the state of Wei.

Ji Kangzi and the Duke Ai of Lu treated Confucius as a state treasury, from whom to seek advice. Once Duke Ai asked Confucius, "what must I do so that common people will look up to me?" Confucius said, "if you promote the upright people and put them above the crooked people, then common people will look up to you. If you promote the crooked and put them above the upright people, then common people will not look up to you" (*Analects* 2.19). Ji Kangzi also asked Confucius for advice several times. Once he asked Confucius how to govern. Confucius answered to govern yourself: when you yourself were correct, others would follow you (*Analects* 12.17). Another time, Ji Kangzi complained to Confucius that there were too many thieves and robbers. Confucius told him straightforwardly that this was because Ji Kangzi himself had too many desires (*Analects* 12.18). Still another time, Ji Kangzi asked Confucius whether it was okay to kill bad people, and Confucius told him that there was no need for killing at all if he, the ruler, desired to be good (*Analects* 12.19). Yet another time, Ji Kangzi asked Confucius how to make common people reverent, diligent, and enthusiastic, and Confucius responded, "if you take care of their things seriously, they will be reverent to you; if you love your parents and are kind to children, they will be diligent to you; if you promote the good people and educate the weak-abled, they will be enthusiastic" (*Analects* 2.20). In all these cases, Confucius asked rulers to be exemplars to their people, a point we will examine in some detail in Chapter Four.

While these are all instances of general advice, Confucius also provided advice on concrete matters. Ji Kangzi proposed making changes to the tax law, which essentially would double taxes. He sent Ranqiu to Confucius for his opinion. Confucius told Ranqiu that a superior person ought to be generous in giving but stingy in taking. If so, the existing taxation would already be enough; if one were greedy, then even doubling the tax would not be enough. However, Ji Kangzi did not listen and put the new taxation law into effect anyway. Confucius was angry, thinking it was also Ranqiu's fault, as he was then the manager of the Ji family. Confucius said, "Ranqiu is no longer my student. You, my student, may openly attack him" (*Analects* 11.17). Ranqiu, however, complained: "it was not that I didn't like your teaching but that I was not strong enough" to resist Ji Kangzi. Confucius did not accept this, saying "those who are not strong enough would stop halfway, but you have not even tried to start yet" (*Analects* 6.12).

When Ji Kangzi planned an attack on Zhuanyu 顓臾, he sent Ranqiu and Zilu to Confucius for his opinion. Zhuanyu was an ancient state, currently within and subjected to the state of Lu, and so Confucius thought there was no need to attack it. Asked if it was their idea to attack, Ranqiu replied that it was Ji Kangzi who wanted to attack, while they originally did not. Confucius told them their role to play by first citing an ancient saying, "one should take a position only if one has the capacity to do it; if not, one shall resign," and then explained, "what is the use of an assistant if he does not hold a blind person when the latter encounters danger and is going to fall? You are wrong in what you say. Whose fault would it be if tigers and rhinoceros escape from their cages or tortoise shell and beautiful jade are destroyed in their cases?" Then Ranqiu mentioned reasons to attack Zhuanyu: it had strong city walls and was very close to the house of Ji Kangzi. Confucius replied that Ji Kangzi's real target was not Zhuanyu but Duke Ai of Lu, as he was afraid that Duke Ai would attack his house with support from Zhuanyu (*Analects* 16.1).

However, after his return to Lu, other than continuing to teach his students, his life-long pursuit, Confucius spent most of his time in editing classics, which would eventually become the six Confucian classics. As we mentioned, the main subject of his teaching is classics. In his early teaching career, he focused mainly on the *Book of Poetry*, the *Book of Documents*, the *Book of Rites*, and the *Book of Music*. In his later years, he added the *Book of Change* and the *Spring and Autumn Annals* to his curriculum. In the process of his teaching, he felt it necessary to do some work on them, and left his mark, to different extents, on the five classics we can see today (the sixth one, the *Book of Music*, is no longer extant).

We can perhaps divide Confucius's work on these classics into three categories in terms of how much Confucius contributed to these classics. First, there are texts, perhaps with multiple versions, that existed before Confucius, and his main work was to edit them. This includes the *Book of Poetry*, the *Book of Documents*, and the text part of the *Book of Change*. For example, regarding the *Book of Poetry*, Confucius himself stated that, "since I returned from Wei to Lu, I put music right, with *Ya* 雅 and *Song* 頌 being assigned to their proper places" (*Analects* 9.15). This shows that the two parts of this classic, *Ya* and *Song*, were already in existence. Confucius eliminated duplicate poems and put individual poems into the appropriate category, *Ya* or *Song*. The *Book of Documents* is a collection of political documents from three dynasties, Xia 夏, Shang 商, and Zhou 周. Confucius collected all the political documents and combined them into one single book. As for the text part of the *Book of Change*, Confucius spent a lot of time in his later years studying it, but perhaps he didn't do anything to the text.

Second, there are texts influenced by but completed after Confucius. These include the *Book of Rites* and the commentary part of *the Book of Change*. Rites can be regarded as the most important part of Confucius's teaching. Confucius divided rites into eight categories such as funeral, worship, adulthood, marriage, etc. These rites for Confucius govern both state activities and individual behaviors. So on the one hand, Confucius said that "the state should be governed with rites" (*Analects* 11.26), and on the other hand, he said that one cannot be established if "one does not know rites" (*Analects* 20.3) or "does not learn rites" (*Analects* 16.13). However, there was no *Book of Rites* before Confucius, and the three books of rites, *Zhou li* 周禮, *Yili* 儀禮, and *Liji* 禮記, as we know them today, were formed in the Han dynasty. However, it is believed that Confucius edited *Yili*, and his influence can also been seen in the other two books of rites. In terms of the commentary part, the so-called "Ten Wings," of the *Book of Change*, it did not exist prior to Confucius. It is sometimes believed that Confucius wrote this commentary. This may not be true, but certainly it includes some of Confucius's ideas as communicated to his students.

The third is the text authored by Confucius to a great extent, and this is the case of *Spring and Autumn Annals*. It is possible that Confucius might have used materials from the official history of the state of Lu, but it is believed for several reasons that the *Annals* was written by Confucius. First, it does not include the complete history of the state of Lu. Instead it starts with 722 BCE and ends with 481 BCE, 2 years before Confucius died. Second, it is not exclusively about the state of Lu but also includes important events taking place in other states at the time. Third, the subtle judgments made of the events represent Confucius's ideas. About this last point, Mencius explains that, at Confucius's time, "the world was declining and the way was eclipsed. Distorted theories and cruel actions prevailed. There were ministers killing rulers and sons killing fathers. Confucius was deeply concerned about it, and as a result he wrote the *Spring and Autumn Annals*. Originally it was the ruler's job to write such annals. Confucius said, 'people can understand me perhaps because of this book, and people may blame me perhaps also because of this book'" (*Mencius* 3b9).

The only thing we cannot be certain about is Confucius's contribution to the *Book of Music*, since this book did not exist prior to Confucius and got lost long ago. However, in ancient times, poetry and music were inseparable, as poetry was to be sung as music. So in the statement about his work on poetry cited above, Confucius also mentioned that he put music right. It is thus entirely plausible that Confucius also left his mark on the *Book of Music*.

7. Last years

Confucius's wife died in 482 BCE, when Confucius was 70. His only son, Kong Li, died at the age of 50 and left two sons, one an adult, one not yet born. The younger son, Kong Ji 孔伋, also named Zisi 子思, was instrumental later in developing Confucius's teaching. As a teacher, Confucius treated his son in the same way as he did his other students. He didn't teach him anything that he didn't teach his other students. Once, one of Confucius's students, Chen Kang 陳亢, asked Kong Li whether he learned anything different from his father than the rest of the students did. Kong Li answered no, and further told Chen Kang that twice he passed by when Confucius was standing in the courtyard. Confucius once asked him to study the *Book of Poetry* and another time asked him to study the rites, both of which Confucius also asked his other students to study (*Analects* 16.13). During the years when Confucius was traveling outside of Lu, it was Kong Li who took care of his mother and the whole family. Thinking that he didn't give his son enough while receiving support from him, Confucius often felt guilty.

Only one year after the death of his own son, his most favorite student Yan Hui died at the young age of 41. Confucius treated Yan Hui as his own son, while Yan Hui also regarded Confucius as his father. Yan Hui's family was poor, but he found joy in learning. Confucius once said, "What a worthy person Hui is! With a bowlful of rice and a ladleful of water and living in a shabby lane, other people would not be able to endure, but Hui does not allow this to affect his joy. What a worthy person Hui is!" (*Analects* 6.11). He also said, "if there is anyone who listens to me with unflagging attention, this must be Hui" (*Analects* 9.20).

Confucius encouraged his students to express their own opinions. Although Yan Hui normally did not argue with him and did not appear to be wise, Confucius said, "I speak to Hui all day long without his disagreeing with me in any way. He looks like being stupid. However, when he reflects on matters alone, he does throw light on what I say. He is not stupid at all" (*Analects* 2.9). As a matter of fact, once his student Zigong, known to be smart and full of himself, acknowledged that Yan Hui was smarter than he was, saying that Yan Hui could learn ten things when taught only one, while he himself could only know two things when taught one. Confucius, in his response, claimed that not only Zigong but he himself was not as good as Yan Hui (*Analects* 5.9). Yan Hui was believed to have the quality of being a chief minister of a state, but he was not anxious to seek an official position. For this Confucius praised him, saying that only Yan Hui and he himself could accomplish things when employed and set the ability aside when not employed (*Analects* 7.11).

So the death of such a favorite student of his was indeed saddening to Confucius. When he first heard it, he said, "Alas, Heaven has abandoned me! Heaven has abandoned me" (*Analects* 11.9). Seeing their master so sad, his students asked whether he had shown excessive sorrow, and Confucius replied, "Had I? Yet, if not for Yan Hui, to whom should I show excessive sorrow?" (*Analects* 11.10). However, when it came to the funeral and burial of Yan Hui, Confucius still insisted on ritual propriety. When Yan Hui's father, Yan Lu 顏路, also a student of Confucius, asked whether Confucius could use his carriage to make an exterior coffin, Confucius said that Yan Hui as a common *shi* should be buried with one layer of coffin, and this was also the way he had buried his own son. Moreover, Confucius said that he was a member of the minister class (*dafu* 大夫), and it was against ritual propriety for him to walk on foot for official matters (*Analects* 11.8). He also opposed his students' plan to have a lavish funeral for Yan Hui. When they eventually proceeded with one, Confucius said, "Yan Hui, you looked at me as your father, yet I have been prevented from treating you as my son. This is not done by me but by your fellow students" (*Analects* 11.11).

Again only one year after the death of Yan Hui, Confucius lost his most intimate student, Zilu. Zilu was the oldest and earliest among Confucius's students. He was only a few years younger than

Confucius and had been with him for more than 40 years. Zilu's personality was very different from Yan Hui. He was fully devoted to Confucius and protected him all the time. Confucius once said, "If the Way would not prevail and I had to go abroad on a raft, the one who would follow me must be Zilu" (*Analects* 5.7). Zilu was also known to be frank. As we have seen above, there were more than a few times when he openly disagreed with Confucius, but he was also willing to change his mind when his mistakes were pointed out. He was the closest to Confucius. Confucius also acknowledged his superior governing abilities (*Analects* 5.8, 6.8, and 11.24). Indeed, among Confucius's students, Zilu was one of those who assumed the most and the highest government positions. One of his obvious shortcomings was being brave without careful judgment, for which Confucius criticized him (*Analects* 5.7, 7.11, and 11.22) and worried that he might not have a good death (*Analects* 11.13), which unfortunately turned out to be true. After returning to Lu, Zilu first served in the Ji Family. Then in 481 BCE, he went to the state of Wei, serving as the governor of the town of Kong Li 孔悝, the chief minister for Duke Chu of Wei. In a coup by the exiled Kuaikui, Zilu went alone to save Kong Li, held in custody by soldiers of Kuaikui. Hopelessly outnumbered, Zilu was killed and cruelly ground. Before he died, he put on his hat, saying that a superior person would not die without a hat. Hearing of this, Confucius became extremely sad and could not eat for many days.

Soon Confucius himself became sick and did not recover. On April 11, 479 BCE, Confucius died at age 73. His students held a funeral for him. Many people came, including Duke Ai of Lu. After the funeral, his students continued to mourn him for 3 years, as they would do for their own parents. When the 3-year period was over, and other students left, Zigong built a hut next to Confucius's tomb and mourned for additional 3 years. Later, a number of Confucius's students as well as a few other people of Lu built their homes near Confucius's tomb and formed a Confucian neighborhood. The state of Lu used Confucius's residence as a temple in his commemoration. These are the so-called three Kongs (Kong Tomb, Kong Neighborhood, and Kong Temple) that still exist today in Confucius's hometown, Qufu of Shandong province.

8. Conclusion

After Confucius died, Confucianism developed into eight different schools, most important of which were the school of Mencius (371–289 BCE) and that of Xunzi (298–238 BCE). Confucius's most important teachings are on humanity and rules of propriety, and Mencius developed the former, while Xunzi focused on the latter. The most important disagreement between the two is their view of human nature, as Mencius claimed it is good, while Xunzi argues that it is bad. This disagreement, though, is partially due to their different understandings of human nature. Mencius understands it to be what distinguishes humans from animals, while Xunzi regards it as the natural tendency human beings are born with. In the first two unified dynasties after the warring states period, Confucianism faced two strikingly contrasting destinies. The Qin dynasty (221–206 BCE) adopted the Legalist ideas of government. In order to exclude heresies, with Confucianism as its primary target, it initiated the notorious "burning of books and burying of Confucians." The Han dynasty (206–220 BCE), in contrast, adopted the policy of "promoting Confucianism and banning all other schools." Confucianism thus became the state ideology, and Dong Zhongshu (179–140 BCE) was the most important representative of Confucianism in this period. In the ensuing periods, with the rise of Neo-Daoism, the so-called learning of the mysterious (*xuanxue*), as well as the Daoist religion, and the introduction of Buddhism into Chinese, Confucianism lost its monopoly, which it regained in the Song Dynasty (960–1279), with the rise of Neo-Confucianism, normally regarded as the second main stage in the development of Confucianism, which continued until the beginning of the Republic era (1911). The unique feature of Neo-Confucianism is to meet the challenge of Daoism and Buddhism, which are both strong in metaphysics, by providing a metaphysical foundation for classical Confucian moral values, partially by drawing on the very resources of Daoism and Buddhism. There are two main schools of Neo-Confucianism, the school of principle, with Zhu Xi (1130–1200) as its greatest synthesizer, and the school of heart–mind, with Wang Yangming (1472–1528) as its culminating figure. The influence of Neo-Confucianism went beyond China to other East Asian countries such as Japan, Korea, and Vietnam. In the Republican period, Confucianism was criticized as the root source of the weakness and backwardness of China under the threat of modern Western powers; and in much of the communist rule since 1949, Confucianism was rejected as the ideology of Chinese feudalism, the target of the communist revolution. It was in Hong Kong and Taiwan that we saw the third stage in the development of Confucianism, the so-called Contemporary New Confucianism, marked by the historical "Manifesto on Chinese Culture" by Zhang Junmei, Xu Fuguan, Tang Junyi, and Mou Zongsan on January 1, 1958. The main task of Contemporary New Confucianism is to meet the challenge from the West by arguing for the compatibility of Confucianism with science and democracy. Such a tendency has been developing in mainland China since the 1980s.

CHAPTER TWO

Morality: Why you should not turn the other cheek

1. Introduction

What is the appropriate attitude toward wrongdoers? Jesus famously said, "You have heard that it was said, 'An eye for an eye, and a tooth for a tooth.' But I tell you, Do not resist an evil person. If someone strikes you on the right cheek, turn to him the other also. And if someone wants to sue you and take your tunic, let him have your cloak as well. If someone forces you to go one mile, go with him two miles" (Matthew 5.39-41). Confucius's teaching is very different. When asked what he thought about the Daoist idea of repaying injury with a good turn as advocated by Laozi in *Daodejing* 49 and 63, Confucius responded: "if so what do you repay a good turn with? You repay an injury with uprightness, but you repay a good turn with a good turn" (*Analects* 14.34). In this chapter, I shall first examine the unique attitude that Confucius recommends to us toward wrongdoers (Section 2). Confucius's answer to our title question is that to turn the other cheek creates an opportunity for the wrongdoer to commit another wrongdoing, which is not good for the wrongdoer. So we shall examine in what sense Confucius believes that it is not in the interest of a person to commit wrongdoing (Section 3). So in Confucius's view, we ought not to turn the other cheek primarily not because we do not want to suffer injustice but because we do not want to leave others in an immoral situation. This raises the question of whether we have a moral duty to makes others virtuous and, if so, how to make others virtuous (Section 4). The chapter concludes with a brief summary (Section 5).

2. Repay injury with uprightness

The exact meaning of Confucius's "repaying injury with uprightness" is subject to scholarly disagreement. While Confucius does
not agree with the attitude that Jesus recommends toward wrongdoers: to repay an injury with a good turn, does he agree with the
attitude that Jesus condemns: to repay an injury with an injury?
Li Ling 李零, a contemporary Chinese scholar, claims that this is
precisely what Confucius means by "repaying injury with uprightness." Li Ling reads the Chinese character, *zhi* 直, here translated
as "uprightness," as *zhi* 值, meaning "value." In this interpretation, what Confucius says is that you ought to repay injury by the
wrongdoers with an injury of equal value, not more or less than
the injury you received. To support his view, he cites what is also
recorded as Confucius's saying in the *Book of Rites*: "with repaying a good turn with a good turn, people can be morally encouraged, and with repaying injury with injury, people will be warned";
and "to repay an injury with a good turn indicates a person of
great lenience, while to repay a good turn with injury indicates a
violent person" (*Liji* 32.6). In Li Ling's view, Confucius advocates
the two attitudes in the first group and condemns the two attitudes
in the second group (Li Ling 2007: 262).

While there is some plausibility with this interpretation, it is not
plausible after all. First, while the character which means "uprightness" can indeed also mean what the character with the additional
radical of "person" to the left of it means, that is, "value," the
character without the radical is a central concept, appearing 22
times in 16 different chapters of the *Analects*. In none of these
other places, some of which we shall examine more closely below,
can it possibly mean "value." Second, if Confucius really means
to say to "repay injury with an injury," it would be much simpler
and rhetorically more effective for him to say it directly, instead of
using the character that can mean "value." Third, if the character should indeed be read as value, and Confucius indeed thinks
that we should repay the wrongdoers the equal value of what they
have done to us, then perhaps Confucius would similarly recom-
mend that we should repay the virtuous persons the equal value of
what they do to us. Thus, instead of two slogans, to repay a good
turn with a good turn and to repay injury with *zhi* (equal value),

Confucius would have used one single slogan: to repay anything with *zhi* (equal value). Of course, we know that Confucius does not do that.

According to a relatively more popular and perhaps more plausible interpretation, adopted by Li Zehou 李澤厚 among many others, repaying injury with uprightness is an attitude toward wrongdoers that occupies a middle position, in terms of moral demandingness, between repaying injury with injury and repaying injury with a good turn. While repaying injury with an injury is morally too permissive and repaying injury with a good turn is morally too demanding, repaying injury with uprightness is morally realistic or practicable. Li Zehou supports his interpretation by citing Kang Youwei's 康有為 commentary on this *Analects* passage: "Confucius's teaching is not far from humans as they are . . . and is something that everyone can practice. It is not that Confucius does not like a high standard, but that, when high and deep, such standard can only be practiced by one or two persons and not by everyone, and for this reason, it cannot be the great way" (in Li Zehou 1999: 339). Here the term "uprightness" is understood to mean "what one really feels" without attempt to cover it. This sense of "uprightness" seems to be consistent with another appearance of the same character in the *Analects*. It is about a person, Weisheng Gao 微生高, who was asked by someone for some vinegar. As he did not have any, he asked his neighbors for some and then gave it to the person. In this *Analects* passage, Confucius says that Weisheng Gao is not an upright person (*Analects* 5.24).[1]

This interpretation is also problematic. It assumes that, even for Confucius, to repay injury with a good turn is a higher moral standard than to repay injury with uprightness, and Confucius promotes the latter only because the former is too difficult for people to practice. This assumption is wrong, as I shall argue presently that to repay injury with uprightness is a much higher standard than to repay injury with a good turn. Moreover, understood as acting according to what one truly feels, "to repay injury with uprightness" becomes morally empty. If I am a bad person myself, when someone causes me harm, I may truly feel that I ought to take revenge, most likely causing more harm to the person than the person harms me. Would Confucius thus endorse my action simply because it comes from my true feeling?

Clearly, crucial to our understanding of Confucius's advice regarding our attitude toward wrongdoers is the Chinese character translated here as "uprightness," and so it is helpful to take a look at some of the other appearances of the same character in the *Analects* to understand what it means. In one place, after stating that he never condemns or praises anyone unless he has tested the person, Confucius says that people in the three dynasties, Xia, Shang, and Zhou, Confucius's ideal societies, did exactly the same, and "so they practiced the way of uprightness" (*Analects* 15.25). Here clearly, uprightness does not mean to act from what one feels but to act in a way that is appropriate to the person in question: if one praises a person who deserves praise and condemns a person who deserves condemnation, one acts uprightly. In other words, to be upright is to stick to the moral standard about what is right and what is wrong. An important goal of Confucian moral cultivation is to fully realize or complete or accomplish oneself (*da* 達). Asked when a person can be regarded as accomplished, Confucius mentions three things, the first of which is "to be upright in character and fond of morality" (*Analects* 12.20).

For Confucius, uprightness is only one of the virtues and so cannot be properly understood in separation from others. In the *Analects*, Confucius mentions two of them: learning and propriety. Confucius states that a person fond of uprightness and yet not of learning or propriety tends to be acrimonious to people (*Analects* 8.2 and 17.8). So a truly upright person is not acrimonious, which is echoed by Zigong, one of Confucius's students, when he says that one type of person he does not like is "people who mistake exposing others' wrongdoing for uprightness" (*Analects* 17.24). So an upright person is not merely a person who says or does things according to whatever he or she feels; rather it is a person who always says and does the right thing. More concretely, as Xunzi, an early exponent of Confucianism, points out, "the virtue of uprightness means to regard what is right as right and what is wrong as wrong" (*Xunzi* 2.3). For this reason, a person who acts uprightly sometimes may need to overcome what he or she actually feels in his or her heart, if what he or she feels is not a morally right thing. Of course, a truly virtuous person, such as Confucius after he turns 70, will always feel the right thing, and so the person will always act uprightly if he or she does so according to what he or she feels in his heart. Clearly this requires a long process of moral self-cultivation, an important aspect of which is what neo-Confucians mean by "training one's feelings according to human nature" (*xing qi qing* 性其情), in contrast to "letting one's feeling control human nature" (*qing qi xing* 情其性).

So to repay injury with uprightness really means to treat wrongdoers morally. But this interpretation is too ambiguous to be of any practical use: what should we do toward wrongdoers if we want to do the morally right thing? One way to understand it is to see how Confucius contrasts the term uprightness with its opposites. Confucius makes a contrast between uprightness and deceptiveness. In one place, he says that "ancient people who were not smart were nevertheless upright, while contemporary people who are not smart are deceptive (*zha* 詐)" (*Analects* 17.16). In another place, he says that "uprightness makes it possible for a person to live, and a deceptive (*wang* 罔) person can live a life only with a good luck of escaping the damage" (*Analects* 6.19). So what contrasts an upright person is a deceptive person and not one who does not hold what he or she feels inside. This passage has an additional implication: it is not in the interest of the person to be deceptive in particular or immoral in general, or, to put it in another way, it is in the interest of a person to be upright, an implication of particular significance that I shall discuss below.[2]

However, a truly upright person does not merely act from self-interest. This can be seen from the contrast Confucius makes between uprightness and crookedness (*wang* 枉). Confucius says that "promoting the upright person above the crooked person can make the crooked person upright" (*Analects* 12.22). In this same *Analects* passage, his student Zixia illustrates what Confucius means by saying that when sage Kings Shun and Tang promoted upright persons Gaoyao and Yin Yi, respectively, there were hardly people lacking in humanity, as people originally lacking in humanity were made upright by Gaoyao and Yin Yi. Zixia certainly got Confucius right, as it can be confirmed by the fact that Confucius praised Shi Yu 史魚, an upright minister in the state of Wei. Shi Yu, about to die, told his son that he had not been able to persuade his boss, King Ling of Wei, to promote the worthy Ju Boyu and demote the unworthy Mi Zixia. Therefore, his funeral should not be held in the main hall but only in a side room. Soon he died and his son did as instructed. King Ling of Wei asked why, and his son told him what his father said to him. Hearing this, the king finally accepted the advice, promoting Ju Boyu and demoting Mi Zixia. This is the famous story of "remonstration with a corpse (*shijian* 屍諫)" in Chinese history, and Shi Yu was regarded as a person who not only made himself upright (*zhi ji* 直己) but also made the other (King Ling of Wei) upright (*zhi ren* 直人). With this double sense of uprightness in mind, Confucius exclaimed, "How upright Ziyu was indeed!" (*Analects* 15.7).[3] Here we see the unique feature of uprightness: a person with the virtue of uprightness is not only upright himself or herself but one who makes others upright. This is a feature of uprightness that is highlighted by Confucius's follower, Mencius. While saying that "a person who is not upright himself or herself cannot make others upright" (*Mencius* 3a1), Mencius emphasizes that an upright person makes nonupright persons upright (*Mencius* 3a4). It is also confirmed by a statement in the *Zuo's Commentary on the Spring and Autumn Annals*: "To right the crooked is called uprightness" (*Zuozhuang*: Duke Xiang, Year 7).

With the term uprightness understood this way, what precisely does Confucius advise us to do toward wrongdoers when he asks us to repay injury with uprightness? For example, when someone strikes me on the cheek, should I turn the other cheek or should I fight back? Confucius perhaps would not exclude either option absolutely. Confucius would approve them if they are truly conducive to making the wrongdoer cease to be a wrongdoer. On the one hand, to fight back, that is, to repay injury with injury as a punishment, as we have seen, for Confucius, may warn the wrongdoer against or deter him or her from committing wrongdoing again. However, its effectiveness is highly questionable. First, punishment can perform the function of deterrence better when it is carried out by a neutral party, government for example. Punishment by the victim, even if rightly, will mostly likely be seen, particularly by the wrongdoer, as retaliation, which tends to invite the wrongdoer to commit further wrongdoing. Second, while Confucius does not exclude punishment as a governmental function, he is also highly skeptic of its effectiveness and significance (see *Analects* 2.3). On the other hand, to turn the other cheek, that is, to repay injury with a good turn, as we have also seen, for Confucius, may indicate a person of great lenience. If the victim simply wants to show his own virtue, which might be the case with Jesus's teaching,[4] this is not something that Confucius would approve. However, Confucius could approve it if the victim's virtuous action is at least partially meant to transform the wrongdoer.[5] While Confucius does put a lot of emphasis on the importance of exemplary action in moral education, he does not advise us to endure whatever harm the wrongdoer is going to inflict upon us, not only for our own well-being but also for the well-being of the wrongdoer, as he perhaps is afraid that our willing acceptance of, or even offer to receive, the injury from the wrongdoer may encourage the person to continue to do it, just as our repaying a good turn to a good turn can encourage the good person to continue to do good.

Confucius's view may be better illustrated in the following anecdotal story. Zeng Sen, a student of Confucius, famous for his virtue of filial piety, once harmed plants while weeding. His father became excessively angry and hit him so hard with a large stick that Zeng Sen was knocked unconscious. After recovering, he went to his father, saying that he deserved the punishment and expressing worry that in hitting him, his father might have been exhausted. Then he went to his room to sing and play the zither, to show his father that he was fine. Zeng Sen thought that he was practicing filial piety as his master has taught him, and so he related what happened to Confucius. Instead of praising Zeng Sen, however, Confucius blamed him, asking him to learn from Shun, the legendary sage king who was also famous for his virtue of filial piety.

Shun's mother died when he was very young. His father remarried and had a son, Xiang, with his new wife. All three hated Shun, frequently causing him trouble and even attempting to kill him. Shun was still very filial to his parents and loved his brother. He did all the chores for the family and was willing to accept appropriate punishments when he made mistakes. However, he made sure that he would not let his parents kill him in their several attempts. Once, his father asked him to repair the roof of the grain store. When Shun was on the roof, his brother took the ladder off and set fire to the grain store. However, Shun managed to escape the disaster, using his bamboo hat as a parachute. Another time, his stepmother asked him to dig a well. When it was deep, she asked her son, Xiang, to dump the dirt in, attempting to bury Shun alive in the well. However, Shun had dug a tunnel in advance and escaped another disaster.

Confucius explains that Shun tried to avoid being killed by his parents and brother not because he was scared of death but because if he allowed them to succeed, they would have done something immoral. So by escaping being killed, Shun actually helped prevent his parents from committing evil acts. Confucius told Zeng Sen that, to follow the example of Shun, when his father intended to hit him so hard for such a minor fault, which was obviously wrong, Zeng Sen should have gotten away, so that his father would not have the opportunity to commit this wrongdoing, and he would not put his father in an immoral situation (*Kongzi Jiayu* 15; 103).

This is perhaps the most famous line in this equally famous story: to put your father in an immoral situation (*xian qi fu yu buyi* 陷其父於不義), whose philosophical significance has not been fully recognized, even though it has become a common phrase among contemporary Chinese. What is particularly revealing in this line is that one's action or inaction can not only make the agent himself or herself a moral or immoral person but may also make others (and consequently and ultimately the agent himself or herself as well) a moral or immoral person. By turning the other cheek, we might think that we are showing our perfection in character. However, by doing so, we have created or at least not tried to eliminate the opportunity for the person to commit a(nother) wrongdoing. In other words, our action puts the other person in an immoral situation or makes the person immoral.[6]

Of course, in the case of turning the other cheek, we only allow the person to hit us. So while it is still our responsibility, according to Confucius's high standard, to eliminate such opportunities for others to do wrong things, we may still think that at least we have not done anything positive to invite the person to hit us: the person wants to hit us and we simply don't resist. However, we may also put another person in an immoral situation simply because we eliminate or fail to create an opportunity for the person to do moral things. This is the moral implied in another anecdotal story. Another student of Confucius, Zilu, was the governor of Pucheng, a small town. There was a flood, and he led people to build dams and dig ditches. Seeing the people were all hungry, he gave everyone a basket of food from his own household. Hearing this, Confucius immediately sent another of his students, Zigong, to ask Zilu to stop. Zilu didn't understand, as he thought he was practicing precisely the way of humanity that his master taught him. Confucius explained to Zilu that, if he saw people were hungry, he should report it to the duke of his state, who was supposed to then open the grain store of the state. By giving out his own food, Zilu actually put the duke in an immoral situation, as he eliminated the opportunity for the duke to take his moral responsibility or created an opportunity for his duke to be irresponsible (*Kongzi Jiayu* 8; 41).

As we can do something to put others in an immoral situation, we can also do something to put others in a moral situation, by helping them to correct wrong deeds done, as seen from yet another anecdotal story, mentioned in the previous chapter. One of the things that Confucius did when he was the assistant minister of public works in the state of Lu was to change the arrangement of the tombs of the deceased dukes. After Duke Zhao of Lu died in exile, his body was taken back to the state of Lu but was buried south of the tombs of the previous dukes, separated by a road, in order to degrade Duke Zhao. This was done by the then chief minister Ji Pingzi, the father of the current chief minister Ji Huanzi, whom Confucius was serving. Confucius persuaded Ji Huanzi that, by improperly degrading Duke Zhao this way, his father himself committed the ritual impropriety. By changing it, his father, and therefore his family, would be freed from the charge of ritual impropriety. So Confucius got permission from Ji Huanzi to dig a ditch south of the tomb of Duke Zhao so that it was with the other tombs of deceased dukes of Lu, as they were now all to the north of the ditch.

So precisely what does Confucius advise us to do toward wrongdoers when he asks us to repay injury with uprightness? The answer is to do whatever is upright, that is, whatever can make the wrongdoer cease to be a wrongdoer or, to put it in a more positive way, make the nonupright person upright.

3. Why it is not in the interest of a person to be immoral

It is important to emphasize that in all the above stories about what to do toward wrongdoers, Confucius is primarily concerned with the well-being of the wrongdoers. Of course the well-being in question here is the person's internal well-being, which is more important than a person's external well-being. This ranking between the two different types of well-being is similar to what Aristotle says when he distinguishes between the genuine sense of self-lover and the vulgar sense of self-lover. In his view, a virtuous person is not only a self-lover but one who loves himself most. He points out that we often "ascribe self-lover to people who assign to themselves the greater share of wealth, honours, and bodily pleasures" (Aristotle: 1168b15–17); however, in Aristotle's view, a person who is "always anxious that he himself, above all things, should act justly, temperately, or in accordance with any other of the virtues . . . would seem more than the other a lover of self; at all events he assigns to himself the most authoritative element in himself and in all things obeys this" (Aristotle: 1168b25–31). Although both a wicked man and a virtuous man are self-lovers, Aristotle argues that the former is reproachable, while the latter is laudable: "the good man should be a lover of self (for he will both himself profit by doing noble acts, and will benefit his fellows), but the wicked man should not; for he will hurt himself and his neighbours, following as he does evil passions" (Aristotle: 1069a12–15). It is important to note that, when Aristotle says that a good man both profits by doing noble acts and benefits his fellows, he is saying that, by doing noble acts, the person profits himself in his internal well-being and benefits others in their external well-being. In contrast, when he says that a wicked man will hurt himself and his neighbors, he is saying that the person hurts himself in his internal well-being and hurts others in their external well-being.

However, Confucius diverts from Aristotle in two important aspects. I shall discuss the first in this section and the second in the next section. The question I shall discuss in this section is in what sense a person's internal well-being is more important than his or her external well-being, and so it is in the genuine interest of a person to be moral and not in the interest of the person to be immoral, even though being moral may require one to make some sacrifice of his or her external well-being, and being immoral can often contribute to the person's external well-being. As is well known, Aristotle attempts to answer this question in his so-called function argument. According to this argument, the good and the "well" of anything that has a function or activity must reside in its unique function. So the good and the "well" of human beings must also reside in the uniquely human function, which is characteristic of human beings or, to use McDowell's term, it is the business of human beings to perform. Aristotle ascertains that this human function is the "active life of the element that has a rational principle" (Aristotle: 1098a3), a good human being is one who performs this unique human function well or excellently, and this excellence of performance of the human function is what he means by virtue. Thus virtue is what makes a person a good human being, a human being who performs rational activities, or lives a rational life, excellently.

Bernard Williams, for one, has consistently argued against such a view. In an early work, he claims that "if it is a mark of a man to employ intelligence and tools in modifying his environment, it is equally a mark of him to employ intelligence in getting his own way and tools in destroying others" (Williams 1971: 73–74). In a response to the Aristotelian defense, Williams maintains that "the life of a wicked or self-indulgent person is equally a certain kind of life structured by reason; it is also a distinctive kind of *human* life. So far we still wait for the considerations that may move the idea of a life 'structured by reason' in the specific direction of life of moderation" (Williams 1995: 199). Williams's suspicion is shared by John McDowell. To illustrate his point that rationality does not lead to virtue, in an essay arguing against Aristotelian naturalism, McDowell imagines a rational wolf. Without reason, the wolf would find it natural for him to play his part in the cooperative activity of hunting with the pack. However, "Having acquired reason, he can contemplate alternatives; he can step back from the natural impulse and direct critical scrutiny at it . . . and frame the question 'why should I do this?'. . . wondering whether to idle through the hunt but still grab his share of the prey" (McDowell 1998: 171). In McDowell's view, even if the wolf by its nature does what virtue might require it to do, the addition of reason may cause it to question its natural behavior. Then, McDowell draws the lesson: "even if we grant that human beings have a naturally based need for the virtues, in a sense parallel to the sense in which wolves have a naturally based need for cooperativeness in their hunting, that need not cut any ice with someone who questions whether virtuous behaviour is genuinely required by reason" (McDowell 1998: 173).[7]

Confucius also attempts to answer this question from his conception of what is uniquely human in his view about the distinction between human being and beast (*ren qin zhi bian* 人禽之辨). He parts company with Aristotle, however, on what is uniquely human. In contrast to the Aristotelian conception, which has become a commonplace in the Western philosophical tradition, that regards rationality as the distinguishing mark of being human, Confucius began a tradition in which humans are distinguished from beasts not in terms of their rationality but in terms of virtues.

Of course, to say that Confucius regards human beings as essentially moral beings is not without controversy, particularly if we assume that the question about the uniqueness of human being and the question about *xing* 性, normally translated as human nature, are identical. Between Confucius's two most able followers in the classical period, Mencius and Xunzi, there was a debate on this issue, with the former claiming that human nature is good and the latter arguing that it is bad. In the only relevant use of the term *xing* in the *Analects*, Confucius says that "humans are alike by their nature and become different through practice" (*Analects* 17.2). Since Confucius does not say in what sense humans are alike by nature, it is sometimes believed that Confucius either does not have a view about whether human nature is good or bad (Ye 1977: 294) or holds a view that regards human nature as neutral with respect of its being good or bad (Chen Daqi 1969: 298).

This is a misunderstanding. If we are talking about a normative conception of human nature to refer to what is uniquely human, then even though Confucius does not say clearly that it is good, it is undoubtedly his view. He emphasizes the difference between humans and beasts: "I cannot be companions of birds and beasts. If I am not going to be companion with human beings, with whom should I be a companion?" (*Analects* 18.6). Moreover, for Confucius, humans are distinguished from beasts by their moral quality, which he calls *ren* 仁, humanity. According to Xu Fuguan 徐復觀, a contemporary Confucian, in the Spring and Autumn period, during which Confucius lived, ritual propriety was considered the distinguishing mark of the human world (Xu 1999: 69). Indeed, it is stated in the *Book of Rites* that "parrots can talk and yet cannot thereby separate them from flying birds; and orangutans can also talk and yet cannot thereby separate themselves from beasts. If humans lack the ritual propriety, even though they can talk, don't they have anything more than the heart of the beast?" So humans are distinguished from beasts because humans have ritual propriety (*Liji* 1.6). In the *Zuo Commentary on the Spring and Autumn Annals*, it is also claimed that "ritual propriety is constitutive of humans" (*Zuozhuan* (*Zuo Commentary*): Duke Zhao, Year 7).

Ritual propriety is also an important idea for Confucius. However, Confucius argues that there is something more fundamental than ritual propriety, which is humanity or humaneness. He asks, "what is the use of ritual propriety if a human being does not have the virtue of humanity?" (*Analects* 3.3). It is important to point out that here the Chinese character for human being, 人, and the Chinese character for the virtue of humanity, 仁, are pronounced the same as *ren*. Moreover, the Chinese character for the virtue of humanity consists of a radical of human being in the left and the character for the number "2" in the right, indicating it is about human relationship. So for Confucius, what distinguishes human beings from beasts is that humans possess the virtue of humanity, and it is in this sense that he claims that "the virtue of humanity is constitutive of human beings" (*Zhongyong* 20). Here he sees humanity as a defining feature of human beings.

In this respect, I agree with Xu Fuguan 徐復觀. In his study of the Pre-Qing theories of human nature, Xu argues that Confucius actually holds the view of human nature as good, because "Confucius believes that humanity is inherent in every human life. It is for this reason that he can say, 'Is humanity far away? It is here as soon as I desire it' [*Analects* 7.30] and 'to practice humanity depends upon oneself' [*Analects* 12.1]. . . . Since Confucius believes that humanity is inherent in every human life, although he does not explicitly say that humanity is human nature . . . he actually believes that human nature is good" (Xu 1999: 97–8). Tang Junyi, another influential contemporary Confucian, also argues that Confucius holds the view that human nature is good: "Confucius says that humans are born with uprightness [*Analects* 6.19], that humanity is here whenever I desire it [*Analects* 7.30], that a humane person can feel at home in humanity [*Analects* 4.2]. . . . So it is appropriate to think that he regards the human heart–mind as the place where good human nature resides. His claim that humans are relatively similar by nature is no different from Mencius's claims that 'things of the same kind are relatively similar' and that 'sages and I are of the same kind.' They all mean that human nature is good" (Tang 1991: 31).

So although Confucius does not directly say that human nature is good, his view of humanity as constitutive of human beings shows clearly that he does hold the view that what distinguishes humans from beasts is that humans possess the virtue of humanity. Humans are alike by their nature, because they all possess humanity, and they grow apart from each other through practice, because some keep it and some abandon it. Mencius is paraphrasing what Confucius says here, when he claims that "the difference between humans and beast is very slight. Superior people keep them [humanity and rightness], while inferior people abandon them" (*Mencius* 4b19). What Mencius does is simply develop an explicitly normative concept of human nature to explain Confucius's idea. In explaining the slight thing that distinguishes not only between humans (that have it) and beasts (that do not have it) but also between superior persons (who preserve it) and inferior persons (who abandon it), Mencius claims that it is the heart–mind of humanity and propriety. On the one hand, "superior persons are different from other people because they preserve their heart–mind. They preserve their heart–mind with humanity and propriety. A person of humanity loves others, and a person of propriety respects others" (*Mencius* 4b28); on the other hand, if a person treats, in an outrageous way, a person of humanity and propriety, who has done his best to the person, then "such a person does not know what he or she is doing. Such a person is no different from beast, and one cannot expect such a person to know any better" (*Mencius* 4b28). Thus, in Mencius's view, while it is important that people be well fed, warmly clothed, and comfortably lodged, sages realize that, "without education, they will become almost no different from animals"; and for this reason sages make sure that people are "taught about human relationships: love between father and son, rightness between ruler and minister, distinction between husband and wife, proper order between older and younger brothers, and faithfulness between friends" (*Mencius* 3a4). This is because, according to Mencius, "everyone has the heart that cannot bear to see the suffering of others. . . . Whoever is devoid of the heart of compassion is not human; whoever is devoid of the heart of shame is not human, whoever is devoid of the heart of courtesy and modesty is not human, and whoever is devoid of the heart of right and wrong is not human" (*Mencius* 2a6).

The difference between Confucius and Mencius lies in their different foci when they use the term "human nature," or "*xing*." While Mencius uses it to refer to what is uniquely human, Confucius uses it to refer to what humans are born with. To put it another way, as Qian Mu points out, Confucius is comparing human beings with human beings, while Mencius is contrasting human beings with beasts (Qian 2005a: 444). However, they both agree that what sets human beings apart from other beings is their moral quality. In this respect, Xunzi, another important follower of Confucius, also agrees, even though he is often regarded as a rival of Mencius, as he argues, directly against Mencius, that human nature is bad, and it is often debated whose view is closer to that of Confucius.

There are two passages in the *Xunzi* that are directly relevant to our question. In one place, Xunzi states that "water and fire possess vital force (*qi* 氣) but lack life. Grasses and trees possess life but lack consciousness. Birds and beast possess consciousness but lack the sense of rightness. Humans possess not only vital force, life, and awareness, but also the sense of rightness. For this reason, humans are the noblest beings of all" (*Xunzi* 9.19). In another place, Xunzi answers the question of what it is that makes one a human being: "a human being is a human being not simply because it is a biped and is featherless, but because it can discriminate [between right and wrong]. Therefore, while birds and beasts have parents and children, there is no affection between them; while they are either male or female, they don't have proper separation between them" (*Xunzi* 5.9).

In both passages, Xunzi makes it clear that humans are distinguished from beasts by their moral quality. This is not contradictory with his better-known view about the badness of human nature. First, he does not use the term *xing* (translated as human nature) in the same sense as Mencius to express the unique feature of human beings in contrast to other beings. What he means by it is rather the natural tendencies that human beings are born with. Second, while the two Chinese characters for the title of the chapter in which Xunzi explicitly discusses the badness of human nature, *xing e* 性惡, are often translated and understood as "Human Nature Is Evil," as De Bary has recently pointed out, it can also be translated and understood as "the badness in human nature" (de Bary 2011: 2) or, more appropriately, the badness in humans' natural tendencies.

The advantage of this new understanding of the chapter title in the *Xunzi* is that it also allows the existence of goodness in humans' natural tendencies, which Xunzi clearly also affirms in his very argument about the badness of human nature. At the beginning of the chapter, Xunzi argues that "a natural tendency that humans are born with is to love profit; when this natural tendency is followed, aggression and greediness arise, while *courtesy* and *deference* disappear. A natural tendency that humans are born with is to have envy and hatred; when this natural tendency is followed, violence and crime occur, while *loyalty* and *trustworthiness* disappear. A natural tendency that humans are born with is to desire to have pleasing sounds and colors; when this natural tendency is followed, dissolute and wanton behaviors occur, while *ritual propriety*, *moral sense*, *gentleness*, and *conscience* disappear" (*Xunzi* 23.2; italics added). Clearly, what disappears must be something that originally exists. So, as de Bary alludes, before humans follow these natural tendencies, they must have courtesy and deference, loyalty and trustworthiness, ritual propriety, moral sense, gentleness, and conscience.

This observation can be supported by two additional pieces of textual evidence in the same chapter. In one place, when he argues against Mencius's view that human nature is originally good but may be lost, Xunzi does not reject Mencius's view about the original goodness of human nature, but argues instead that "it is a natural tendency (*xing*) of humans to deviate from their original simplicity and abandon their natural endowment" (*Xunzi* 23.5), which shows that the original simplicity and natural endowment that Mencius calls the sprouts of moral virtues do originally exist as something humans are born with. In another argument for the badness in humans' natural tendencies, Xunzi claims that we desire what we do not have: as "those who have little desire to have much, those who are ugly desire to be beautiful, those who live in small quarters desire to live in spacious places, those who are poor desire to be rich, and those who are in mean stations desire to be noble," "the fact that humans desire to be good shows the badness in humans' natural tendencies" (*Xunzi* 23.8). What Xunzi tries to show here is that since humans desire to be good, humans lack goodness (if they already have the goodness, humans will not desire it). However, their very desire to be good itself has to be regarded as good.

So a proper understanding of Xunzi's view is that there are both goodness and badness in what humans are naturally born with. As a matter of fact, Xunzi himself states that "humans have both a love for rightness and a desire for profit. Although [sage kings] Yao and Shun cannot make people get rid of their desire for profit, they are able to cause them not to allow their desire for profit to triumph over their love for moral rightness. Although [wicked kings] Jie and Zhou cannot make people get rid of their love for rightness, they are able to cause people not to allow their love for rightness to triumph over their desire for profit" (*Xunzi* 27.67).[8] The reason we praise the sage kings who cause people to develop their love for moral rightness and condemn the wicked kings who do not allow people to do so is that the love for moral rightness is uniquely human, while the desire for profit is common to beasts. Moreover, Xunzi argues that every human being is naturally endowed with the ability to develop the love for moral rightness, and it is in this sense that he claims that everyone can become a sage: "all that makes [sage king] Yu a [sage king] Yu is that he practices humanity, rightness, norms, and rectitude. There is a way to know and to practice them all, and everyone in the street has the faculty to know them and has the faculty to practice them" (*Xunzi* 23. 14).

4. Is a virtuous person supposed to make others virtuous?

What is unique and significant about Confucius, as we have seen, is that, precisely because he realizes that a person's internal well-being is one's true interest, when a truly virtuous person is concerned with the well-being of others, he or she should be more concerned with their internal well-being than their external well-being, especially when the two come into conflict. Turning the other cheek may be conducive to the wrongdoer's external well-being but is certainly detrimental to the person's internal well-being, and it is in this sense that my action of turning the other cheek is immoral and to that degree I am not a genuine virtuous person, who is concerned not only with others' external well-being but, more importantly, also with their internal well-being. In other words, since it is not in the genuine (internal) interest of a person to do immoral things, a moral person, a person who is concerned about others' interest, ought to do all that he or she can to stop the person from doing immoral things.

It is here that I want to highlight the importance of Confucius's teaching in question by contrasting it with virtue ethics in the Western traditions. Virtue ethics has made a significant revival in recent decades, as many people are not satisfied with deontology and utilitarianism, the two dominant moral theories in the modern world. However, one of its serious criticisms, largely made by Kantian philosophers, is that it is self-centered. As summarized by David Solomon, it claims that "an EV [ethics of virtue] tends to focus too much attention on the agent. . . . Such theories demand a focus on the character of the individual agent. What gives the point to the task of acquiring the virtues is that one supposes that one should become a person of a particular kind. . . . This view demands that the moral agent keep his or her own character at the center of his or her practical attention . . . [while] the point of moral reflection essentially involves a concern for others" (Solomon 1997: 169).

Of course, critics of virtue ethics recognize that a virtuous person is concerned about the well-being of others. However, "the objection points to an asymmetry that arises between an agent's regard for his own character and his regard for the character of others. The question raised here has this form: Since an EV [ethics of virtue] requires me to pay primary attention to the state of my own character, doesn't this suggest that I must regard my own character as the ethically most important feature of myself? But, if so, and if I am suitably concerned about others, shouldn't my concern for them extend beyond a mere concern that their wants, needs and desires be satisfied, and encompass a concern for *their* character? Shouldn't I indeed have the same concern for the character of my neighbour as I have for my own?" (Solomon 1997: 172). Solomon uses the example of a Christian's view of love or charity as his or her primary virtue. This person will then make it his or her task to become a person who exhibits this virtue toward others, but this virtue does not require the person to bring it about that others around him or her also exhibit this virtue: "Christian love requires me to attend to the wants, needs and desires of others. But doesn't this suggest that I regard others as less morally important than myself? Satisfying their needs is good enough for them, but I require of myself that I become a loving person" (Solomon 1997: 172).[9]

Aristotle's virtuous person as a true self-lover is also self-centered in this sense, as the virtuous person is one, as we have seen, who is "always anxious that he himself, above all things, should act justly, temperately, or in accordance with any other of the virtues . . . would seem more than the other a lover of self; at all events he assigns to himself the most authoritative element in himself and in all things obeys this" (Aristotle: 1168b25–31). The virtuous person is exclusively concerned with the external well-being of others but is primarily concerned with the internal well-being of his or her self, when the person clearly realizes that the internal well-being is more important and more constitutive of human being than the external well-being. While Aristotle does think that bodily harm and pleasure are real harm and pleasure, he regards them as less important than the harm and pleasure of the soul. Yet, precisely with regard to the harm and pleasure of the soul, Aristotle's virtuous person is only concerned with himself. Moreover, he acquires the pleasure and avoids the harm of his own soul precisely by providing others with bodily pleasure and eliminating or decreasing their bodily harm.[10]

In contrast, Confucius's virtue ethics clearly avoids the self-centeredness objection, as he makes it clear that a virtuous person ought to be concerned with the virtue of others. Confucius once told his students that there is one thread going through all his teachings. After he left, students tried to figure out what this one thread is, and one of his students, Zengzi, said that it is *zhong* 忠 and *shu* 恕 (*Analects* 4.15). According to Yang Bojun, the editor, translator (from classical Chinese to modern Chinese), and annotator of the most authoritative contemporary edition of the *Analects*, the one thread that Confucius says goes through all his teachings is really the Confucian version of the Golden Rule: *Zhong* refers to its positive version: "one who wants to establish oneself shall establish others; and one who wants to prosper oneself shall help others prosper" (*Analects* 6.30), and *shu* refers to its negative version: "do not do unto others what you would not like to be done unto," which is mentioned in several places in the *Analects* (Yang 1980: 39). While there is scholarly disagreement about what *zhong* really means (indeed as far as I know, Yang is the only annotator of the *Analects* who holds this view),[11] there is a basic agreement on what Confucius means by *shu*, as he gives a definition himself precisely in light of what is regarded as the negative version of the Golden Rule (*Analects* 15.24).

However, the debate about what *zhong* really means does not involve us here. Our task is to disclose the unique significance of what have been regarded as the two Confucian formulations of the Golden Rule. The Golden Rule, as commonly understood in the Western tradition, is no more immune to the self-centeredness problem than virtue ethics. Following the Golden Rule, a moral person is supposed to do unto others what one would like to be done unto and not to do upon others what one would not like to be done unto. However, the same person is not required by the Golden Rule, desiring to follow the Golden Rule, to make others also follow the Golden Rule. For example, the Golden Rule requires a person, who desires to be helped by others when in need, to help others in need, but it does not require that the person, for the sake of following the Golden Rule, make others to help (their) others in need; it requires a person, who does not like to be treated unfairly, to not treat others unfairly, but it does not require the person, for the sake of following the Golden Rule, to make others not treat (their) others unfairly. Suppose it is in the interest of a person to follow (and not in the interest of the person to violate) the Golden Rule. The person who follows the Golden Rule in the above sense, just like a virtuous person, is also self-centered.

However, whether you call the *Analects* passage in question the Confucian formulations of the Golden Rule or not, what Confucius means by them clearly avoids the problem of self-centeredness. Let us first examine the so-called positive expression of the Golden Rule. It is true that Confucius does seem to have the external aspect of the Golden Rule in mind when he claims that it is not easy "to serve my father as I would expect my son to serve me. . . . To serve my ruler as I would expect my ministers to serve me. . . . To serve my elder brothers as I would expect my younger brothers to serve me. . . . To be the first to treat friends as I would expect them to treat me" (*Zhongyong* 13). However, he clearly has something more than that in mind in his more famous formulation: Instead of asking us to do unto others as we would like to be done unto, Confucius states: "one who wants to get established (*li* 立) ought to help others get established; and one who wants to get completed (*da* 達) ought to help others get completed" (*Analects* 6.30).

The meaning of *li* is clear enough, to establish or realize oneself, which according to Confucius certainly is more about one's internal character than one's external well-being. When Confucius lists several important landmarks in his life, he mentions that at the age of 30 he established (*li*) himself (*Analects* 2.4). There is no doubt that he is talking about the formation of his character. With regard to the term *da*, Confucius himself provides a definition: "a person of *da* is one who is upright (*zhi*) in character, fond of rightness, sensitive to what other people say, observant of other people's facial expressions, and mindful of being modest" (*Analects* 12.20). All these clearly show that *da* is primarily related to one's inner well-being. Most interestingly, Confucius uses the same term, *zhi* (uprightness), to explain the meaning of *da* as he uses to tell us what to do with the wrongdoers. Since a person of *da* would help others to become *da*, and one essential feature of a person of *da* is being upright, then when Confucius asks us to treat wrongdoers with uprightness, he really means to ask us to make other people also upright, and this is precisely what we have been arguing for.

So while we may continue to regard what Confucius says in *Analects* 6.30 as a version of the Golden Rule, and we may continue to think this Confucian version of the Golden Rule includes the ordinary meaning of the Golden Rule, that is, as we would like to have our own external well-being taken care of, we ought to also take care of other people's external well-being, it is important that we should not ignore its internal aspect, as it is more central to Confucius. Thus, commenting on this *Analects* passage, the greatest neo-Confucian philosopher Zhu Xi states that "the two things [establishing and prospering] include both internal and external" (Zhu 1986: 846). What he means by external is such things as happiness, long life, health, and peace that everyone desires. This is our common understanding of the Golden Rule: since I want to be happy, live long, be healthy, and have peace, I should also help others to be happy, live long, be healthy, and have peace.

What is unique about Zhu Xi's interpretation of the Confucian Golden rule is, however, his emphasis on its internal aspect, which is made clear by the sentence immediately after he talks about the internal and external aspects of the Golden Rule: "Take for example the cultivation of virtue. One wants to get established in one's own virtue," and so, by implication, one should help others get established in their virtues (Zhu 1986: 846). Thus the deeper meaning of the Golden Rule for Zhu Xi is that, if one wants to develop one's own virtue, one should help others develop their virtue; and if one wants to be complete in one's virtues, one should help others be complete in their virtues. This point is made more explicit in another place, where Zhu Xi claims that "what my heart–mind desires is also what the heart–mind of others desire. I want to respect my parents, love my brothers, and be kind [to my children], and so I must also help others respect their parents, love their brothers, and be kind [to their children] as I do to mine. . . . If only I myself can do these, while others cannot do them, I feel uneasy" (Zhu 1986: 363–4). The following statement, made by one of his students in a conversation with Zhu Xi, expresses this internal aspect of the Confucian Golden Rule well: "If one wants to be a superior person, then one also wants all others to be superior persons; if one does not want to be an inferior person, then one also does not want others to be inferior persons" (Zhu 1986: 1071).

The Qing dynasty scholar Mao Qiling 毛奇齡, in his *Corrections of the Four Books* 四書改錯, also interprets this *Analects* passage as to mean that one cannot establish oneself without establishing others, and one cannot make oneself complete without making others complete. In other words, to establish others is intrinsic to establishing oneself and to let others be complete in virtue is intrinsic to making oneself complete in virtue. To use Mencius's term, the self that one is to be concerned with is the great body, the heart–mind with the four inborn sprouts of virtues: humanities, rightness, propriety, and wisdom. For this reason, Mao Qiling relates this passage to the idea of "realizing oneself (*cheng ji* 成己)" and "realizing others (*cheng wu* 成物)" in the *Doctrine of the Mean*, "manifesting one's clear character (*ming mingde* 明明德)" and "loving people (*qin min* 親民)" at the very beginning of the *Great Learning*, "making oneself alone perfect (*du shan qi shen* 獨善其身)" and "making the whole Empire perfect (*jian shan tian xia* 兼善天下)" in *Mencius* 7a9, and "cultivating oneself (*xiu ji* 修己)" and "bringing security to people (*an ren* 安人)" in *Analects* 14.42 (see Cheng Shude: 429). In his view, the two items in each of these pairs are inseparable: one cannot realize oneself without realizing others, manifest one's clear character without loving people, make oneself perfect without making the world perfect, and cultivate oneself without bringing peace to people, and vice versa.

In comparison, it is often believed that Confucius's negative formulation of the Golden Rule is nothing but the Golden Rule in its familiar sense: it is limited to the external aspect. First, in its several appearances in the *Analects*, it simply states: "One ought not to impose upon others what one does not like to be imposed upon oneself," without highlighting the fact that a superior person does not want to be immoral (with the implication that one should therefore help others not to be immoral). In the *Great Learning*, the version of the negative Golden Rule is more concrete, but it appears also to be mainly concerned with the external aspect in mind: "what you do not like the people above to do to you, don't do to people below; what you do not like people in front of you to do to you, do not do to people behind you; what you do not like people behind do to you, do not do to people in front of you; what you do not like people to the right do to you, do not do to people to the left; what you do not like people to the left do to you, do not do to people to the right " (*Daxue* 10). Second, as we have pointed out, Confucius uses this negative formulation of the Golden Rule to explain his idea of *shu*, which he says is the one thread that goes through his teaching. However, one of the literal meanings of *shu* is to forgive. Thus when we see a person doing wrong things, it seems that what we need is simply to forgive the person, instead of trying to help the person cease to do wrong things. However, we would have to help them cease to do wrong things, since we do not want to do wrong things ourselves, should there be an inner aspect in the negative formulation of the Golden Rule. Third, this interpretation seems to get further support from a few other claims of Confucius in the *Analects*: "Be strict with oneself and be lenient with others" (*Analects* 15.15); "the superior person makes demands upon oneself, while the inferior person makes demands upon others" (*Analects* 15.21); while "happy in proclaiming merits of others" (*Analects* 16.5), "the superior person despises those who proclaim faults in others" (*Analects* 17.24); and "attack your own faults, not those of others" (*Analects* 12.21). All these passages seem to suggest that, in his negative formulation of the Golden Rule, Confucius does not require us to help others not do immoral things, even if we do not want to do immoral things ourselves. In other words, this negative formulation of the Golden Rule is only limited to people's external well-being and is not concerned with their internal well-being.

This interpretation, however, cannot be right. On the one hand, thus understood, it cannot be held consistently with Confucius's positive formulation of the Golden Rule, which unmistakably includes and even focuses on our concern with others' internal well-being: since we want to be superior persons, we ought to help others become superior persons. Now, suppose that we want to be superior persons, but there is an inferior person. How can we help the person to become a superior person, as the positive Golden Rule requires us, if we simply forgive or ignore the person's faults and do not demand the person to overcome them? On the other hand, in the *Analects*, there are also a number of passages in which Confucius does say that a virtuous person should be concerned about the internal well-being of inferior people. For example, Confucius states clearly that "I am really concerned about people who fail to cultivate their virtue, don't go deep into what is learned, cannot go in the right direction when pointed out to them, and are unable to correct themselves when they make mistakes" (*Analects* 7.3); "if you love someone, how can you not instruct the person; if you are loyal to someone, how can you not teach the person" (*Analects* 14.7); and "a superior person completes what is good in a person and does not complete what is bad in a person. Inferior person does the opposite" (*Analects* 12.16). But the most important is the passage in *Analects* 4.3, where Confucius says that "only the person with the virtue of humanity knows how to love a person and how to hate a person" (*Analects* 4.3).

This passage is particularly relevant to our interest. First, it shows that a virtuous person not only has people to love but also has people to hate. In other words, a virtuous person does not simply forgive or ignore the moral faults of inferior people. Second, since Confucius elsewhere defines the virtue of humanity as to love people (*Analects* 12.22), clearly, the virtuous person's hating people in this instance, just like the person's loving people, falls under the larger category of love which is constitutive of the virtue of humanity. Third and most important, since in appearance everyone has the ability to love or hate people, and yet Confucius says that only a person with the virtue of humanities knows how to love people and hate people, this shows that, for Confucius, only such a person knows how to love and hate people appropriately.

On the one hand, a virtuous person hates people who ought to be hated, just as the person loves people who ought to be loved. In other words, the virtuous person's hate, just like the person's love, is selfless.[12] In this context, Cheng Yi, a neo-Confucian, compares the heart–mind of a virtuous person with the "bright mirror" and "still water": "when things that should be loved appear, the sage loves them, and when things that should be hated appear, the sage hates them" (Cheng and Cheng 1989: 210–11). In other words, the virtuous person's hate and love are determined by things and not by themselves. In Cheng Yi's view, this is the main distinction between superior persons and inferior persons: "the anger of inferior persons comes from themselves, while the anger of the superior persons comes from things [they are angry at]" (Cheng and Cheng 1989: 306).[13] On this point, his brother Cheng Hao claims that "a sage is happy with something because it is the thing that one should be happy with; a sage is angry with something because it is the thing that one should be angry with. Therefore the heart–mind of a sage is not determined by itself but by external things" (Cheng and Cheng 1989: 460). This interpretation is consistent with what Confucius has in mind. One of his students asks whether a superior person also has people to hate, and Confucius replies: "Yes. A superior person hates those who proclaim faults of others, those who, inferior themselves, slander superior people, those who, though courageous, lack propriety, and those who, while resolute, are stubborn" (Analects 17.24). So a virtuous person only hates vicious people.

On the other hand, while a nonvirtuous person may also hate a vicious person, a virtuous person hates vicious people not in the sense of cursing them or wishing them ill. What is crucial here is that a virtuous person hates a vicious person not simply to express his or her emotion but to express (or not express) his emotion, among other things he or she may do or refrain from doing, in such a way that the vicious person ceases to be vicious. So this Analects passage about a virtuous person's loving and hating people can be understood in tandem with what is said in the Book of Rites: "Loving a person, one ought to know the person's weakness; and hating a person, one ought to see the person's strength" (Liji 1.3).

To see the weakness of the person one loves, one can help the person overcome the weakness, and to see the strength of the person one hates, one will not give up on the person.

If so, how should we understand those *Analects* passages, quoted earlier, in which Confucius seems to say that a virtuous person ought not correct the moral faults of others? While *Shu* does have the meaning of forgiving, it is clear that Confucius does not use it in this sense, as he simply explains that *shu* means to not do unto others what one does not want to be done unto, and not to do unto others what one does not want to be done unto is very different from forgiving other people's wrongdoing. Thus, when asked by a student, regarding this *Analects* passage, whether a person of *shu* ought to forgive other people's moral faults, Zhu Xi says that "this is a strange idea. None of the *Six Classics* ever says that to be *shu* is to be tolerant of others' moral faults. . . . It is not right to take care of oneself only and let other people become bad" (Zhu 1986: 701).

In light of this, we need a different understanding of the *Analects* passages we mentioned above that advise us to be strict with ourselves and lenient with others, make demands upon ourselves and not upon others (*Analects* 15.21), and find faults in ourselves and not in others. What Confucius says is that when a virtuous person encounters a wrongdoer, the virtuous person ought, on the one hand, to reflect how he or she could have done things differently so that the wrongdoer would not be a wrongdoer and, on the other hand, to regard it as his or her own responsibility to renew the wrongdoer so that the person will cease to be a wrongdoer. The *Analects* records a saying, supposedly by King Wu, that illustrates this point very well: "if there are people with moral faults, I am the only person to be responsible" (*Analects* 20.1). So a virtuous person is lenient toward others not because he or she is not concerned with the characters of others, but because he or she regards it his or her responsibility to make others virtuous. So for a virtuous person, the very existence of moral faults in others indicates that he or she has not fully fulfilled his or her responsibility. This point is made most clear by Mencius when he describes Yi Yin: "When he saw a common man or woman who did not enjoy the benefit of the rule of Yao and Shun, Yi Yin felt as if he had pushed him or her into the gutter. This is the extent to which he considered the Empire his responsibility" (*Mencius* 5B1). The neo-Confucian Zhu Xi makes a similar point when he says that "Even if there is one person under heaven who is not touched by their goodness, superior persons will feel somewhat uneasy in their heart–mind; and they realize that they still have something within themselves that has not been fully realized, and so they cannot brighten the [originally] bright [but currently darkened] virtue of all people under heaven. For this reason, although what they do seems to be for the sake of others, as a matter of fact, they are for themselves" (Zhu 1986: 313).

5. Conclusion

In the above, we examined Confucius's view about what to do with wrongdoers. While he does not absolutely exclude the attitude that Jesus condemns, "an eye for an eye" and "a tooth for a tooth," or repay injury with injury, and the attitude that Jesus advocates, turn the other cheek, or repay injury with a good turn, generally speaking he disapproves of both. His principle is that whatever we do should be conducive to the goal of making the wrongdoer cease to be a wrongdoer. To repay injury with injury and to repay injury with a good turn in most cases may both lead to the precisely opposite result, although in different ways: to force or encourage the wrongdoer into further wrongdoing. Instead, Confucius advises us to repay injury with uprightness, first recognizing the immorality of the wrongdoer's actions and then preventing the wrongdoer from committing further wrongdoing by not creating or even eliminating opportunities for them to commit such wrongdoing. We should take this attitude toward wrongdoers for Confucius primarily not for the sake of our own external well-being (so that we will not be further harmed by the wrongdoer) but for the sake of the internal well-being of the wrongdoer (so that he or she will cease to be the wrongdoer). Here Confucius argues that a person's internal well-being is more important than his or her external well-being, as it is the latter that makes a person a human being instead of a beast. Precisely because of this, an appropriate moral attitude toward wrongdoers is not to allow them to commit wrongdoings against us (or anyone else), thereby enhancing the wrongdoer's external well-being, but to stop the wrongdoer from committing wrongdoings, thereby enhancing their internal well-being in the sense that they will become nondefective human beings. Of course, to reach this goal, it is not enough for us just to eliminate or not create opportunities for them to commit wrongdoings; it is also necessary to influence or induce them to be moral persons so that they do not have the desire to commit wrongdoings even if such opportunities present themselves to them. This will be our topic in Chapter Four.

CHAPTER THREE

Virtue: How to love virtue as you love sex

1. Introduction

When we discussed Confucius's life, we mentioned his saying: "I have not seen a person who loves virtue as he loves sex" (*Analects* 9.18). This was a complaint he lodged upon realizing that Duke Ling of Wei was more interested in spending time with his wife, beautiful but with a bad reputation in her private life, than listening to Confucius advise him on how to govern his state with virtues. This is not merely an occasional comment but a central theme in Confucius's teaching in particular and in Confucian moral philosophy in general. For Confucius, it is not enough to do virtuous things; one also needs to love doing them, so that one can do virtuous things joyfully, effortlessly, and with great ease. In this chapter, we shall first examine what he means by loving virtues as loving sex (Section 2), and how it is significant as a plausible answer to the question "why be moral?" (Section 3). We shall then see how Confucius could answer two questions that arise from his discussion of virtues: (1) whether a virtuous person is an egoist in the sense that he or she is concerned about the interest of others only so that he or she can become a virtuous person (Section 4); and (2) whether virtue is paradoxical: on the one hand, virtue is praiseworthy because it is about things that are difficult for humans, but, on the other hand, a virtuous person does such things with great ease (Section 5). The chapter ends with a brief conclusion (Section 6).

2. Taking delight in being moral

The central teaching of Confucius is about moral self-cultivation. However, the highest goal of such self-cultivation is joy (*le* 樂). In several crucial passages in the *Analects*, Confucius expresses this idea most unequivocally. First, Confucius states that "to know it (*zhi zhi* 知之) is not as good as to like it (*hao zhi* 好之); and to like it is not as good as to take delight in it (*le zhi* 樂之)" (*Analects* 6.20). It is not made explicit what this "it (*zhi*)," the object of the three verbs ("know," "like," and "take delight in") in the passage, refers to. However, even though the neo-Confucian interpretation of it as Dao or Principle (*li* 理) may be somewhat controversial, since Confucian learning is primarily a learning about moral cultivation, we can be relatively certain that this "it" must be somewhat related to morality. So what Confucius says here is that to know what is virtuous is not as good as to like what is virtuous, and to like what is virtuous is not as good as to take delight in being virtuous. Even though the neo-Confucian interpretation of the distinction between "like it" (regarding "it" as something external to oneself that one likes) and "take delight in it" (regarding "it" as something one gets from oneself) (see Cheng and Cheng 1989: 361) may be excessively creative, it is also clear that Confucius regards taking delight in being virtuous as the highest stage of one's moral cultivation.

Second, Confucius states that moral cultivation "is to be stimulated (*xing* 興) by poetry, established (*li* 立) by rules of propriety, and accomplished (*cheng* 成) by music" (*Analects* 8.8). As common in classical (and contemporary) Chinese, there is no subject for the three verbs, *xing*, *li*, and *cheng*. However, there is a relative consensus among scholars that what Confucius has in mind is the process of moral cultivation. So in the translation above I assume that what Confucius tries to say is that, in this process, one's moral cultivation starts from reading the *Poetry*, one of the Confucian classics, from which one's moral sentiments can be stimulated; yet such moral sentiments are unstable unless they are regulated by rules of propriety; when one's action is regulated by rules of propriety, one will often have a sense of external force, and so one's moral cultivation can be accomplished only by music, by which one becomes natural in performing moral actions. This interpretation is of course also controversial, but what is not controversial is that Confucius regards "music" as something by which one's moral cultivation is accomplished. To understand this, it is important to point out that not only do music (*yue*) and joy (*le*) share the same Chinese character 樂, but their meanings are also closely related. This is made particularly clear by Confucius's most able follower Mencius: "the essence of music (*yue* 樂) is to take delight (*le* 樂) in the two [humanity (*ren* 仁) and rightness (*yi* 義)], naturally resulting in joy (*le*樂). As soon as the joy arises, it cannot be stopped; as it cannot be stopped, one cannot help but dance with feet and wave with hands even without realizing it" (*Mencius* 4a27). Thus, when one's moral cultivation is accomplished by music, one performs moral actions in the same way as one dances to the music: everything is natural and spontaneous, and one does not feel a slight bit of force or hesitation.

The third is the famous passage in which Confucius describes the milestones of his own moral development in the world's shortest autobiography on record: "at fifteen I set my mind on learning; at thirty I took my stand; at forty I came to be free from doubts; at fifty I understood the decree of Heaven; at sixty my ears are attuned; and at seventy I followed my heart's desire without overstepping the line" (*Analects* 2.4). The meaning of these stages is not entirely clear, but what is most important in this context is the last stage, at which Confucius can act at his heart's desire without violating any moral principles. While the word "joy" (*le*) is not present here, it is a perfect description of what joy means: to act at one's own heart's desire. This is regarded as the highest stage of moral cultivation because at this stage one does not need to worry about any external rules of morality. This of course does not mean that at this stage one has acquired a privileged exemption from the constraints of such rules; rather it means that such rules are no longer needed, as whatever one does, without any consideration of such rules, is precisely what these rules would require one to do. To use Mencius's term, on this stage, one no longer practices humanity and rightness (*xing ren yi* 行仁義) but practices from humanity and rightness (*you ren yi xing* 由仁義行) (*Mencius* 4b19). In the former, humanity and rightness are still seen as something external that one practices; in the latter, however, they are clearly recognized as something internal to oneself. When they are realized as internal, it is indeed close to Confucius's ideal state as indicated by the title of this chapter: love virtue as one loves sex.

Confucius's ideal of loving virtue as one loves sex is also illustrated in two different analogies. In the *Great Learning*, one of the four canons of Confucianism, along with the *Analects*, the *Mencius*, and the *Doctrine of Mean*, one is asked to "love good as one loves the beautiful colors, and hate evil as one hates bad odors" (*Greater Learning* 6). This is a great analogy. One does not need to be told, to make a calculated deliberation, or to make any forced effort, to love beautiful colors and hate bad odors. As soon as one sees beautiful colors, one will love them, and as soon as one smells bad odors, one will hate them. As a matter of fact, one cannot recognize any colors as beautiful until one loves them and cannot regard any odors as bad until one hates them. It is in this sense that Confucius claims that, at this highest stage of moral cultivation, one will "seek to do good as if there is no time left, and avoid doing evil as avoiding touching boiling water" (*Analects* 16.11). In the *Mencius*, the analogy is made between one's sense organ and one's heart–mind: "All palates have the same preference in taste, all ears have the same preference in sound, and all eyes have the same preferences in beauty. How can heart–mind alone be different? In what are all hearts-minds the same? It is principle and rightness. Sages are the first to discover the common thing that pleases our hearts-minds. The principle and rightness pleases (*yue* 悦) my heart–mind just as meat pleases my palate" (*Mencius* 6a7).

To understand this Confucian idea of joy, it is helpful to examine what has been regarded as the joy of Confucius and Yanzi (*kong yan zhi le* 孔顏之樂) in the Confucian tradition. This is related to two passages in the *Analects*. In the first, Confucius praises his student Yan Hui 顏回: "How virtuous is Yan Hui! With a single bamboo dish of food, a single gourd cup of unboiled water, and living on a shabby lane, while all others cannot endure the hardship, only he does not allow his joy to be affected. Yan Hui, how virtuous he is indeed!" (*Analects* 6.11). To live a poor life on a shabby lane is normally considered something painful. Why does Yanzi feel joy in it and why does Confucius praise Yanzi for his finding joy in it? Yanzi is no different from anyone else as poverty cannot make him, just like anyone else, joyful. Obviously Yanzi is joyful and Confucius praises him for some other reason, which is not overridden by the harshness of his life. Then exactly what is the reason? This is made clear in the second *Analects* passage, in which Confucius talks about his own joy: "with coarse grain to eat, with unboiled water to drink, and with my bended arms as pillow—my joy lies right in them. Riches and honors acquired not in a right way seem to me a floating cloud" (*Analects* 7.16). While Confucius praises Yan Hui for not allowing his joy to be affected (*bu gai qi le* 不改其樂) by poverty, he says that he can find joy right in poverty (*le zai qi zhong* 樂在其中). Although some later-Confucian commentators try to emphasize a qualitative difference between Yan Hui's *bu gai qi le* (his joy not being affected by poverty) and Confucius's *le zai qi zhong* (his finding joy in poverty), mainly in order to show that Confucius is on a higher level than Yan Hui, I believe that they are largely describing the same phenomenon.

The reason that Yan Hui's joy is not affected by poverty and Confucius can find joy in poverty is explained in the last sentence of the above *Analects* passage: "riches and honors acquired not in a right way seem to me a floating cloud." Confucius feels joy in, and Yan Hui's joy is not affected by, their poverty because, by not avoiding it, they are abiding by moral principles. Although Confucius says that their joy lies in, or is not affected by, eating coarse grain, drinking unboiled water, and living on a shabby lane, etc., it does not mean that coarse grain, unboiled water, and shabby lanes themselves are good things that provide him with joy. The real source of his joy comes from being in accord with what is virtuous, which would be violated should one try to avoid poverty in these particular cases. This is made clear by a related *Analects* passage: "Riches and honors are what every person desires. However, if they are obtained in violation of *Dao*, they cannot be kept. Poverty and humble stations are what every person dislikes. However, if they can be avoided only in violation of *Dao*, they should not be avoided" (*Analects* 4.5).

On this joy of Confucius and Yanzi (*kong yan zhi le*), Mencius makes a similar point: "Fish is what I want; bear's palm is also what I want. If I cannot have both, I would rather take bear's palm than fish. Life is what I want; rightness is also what I want. If I cannot have both, I would rather take rightness than life. Life is what I want, but there is something that I want more than life. That is why I do not cling to life at all costs. Death is what I hate, but there is something I hate more than death. That is why I do not avoid calamities at all cost" (*Mencius* 6a10). So it is not a morally

bad thing to seek richness and life itself, just as it is not a morally good thing to avoid poverty and death itself. Richness and
life should not be sought after and poverty and death should not
be avoided only if to do so, one must violate moral principle. As
long as one is in accord with moral principles, one can find joy in
anything, whether in poverty or in richness, whether in seeking life
or sacrificing one's life. The description of the joy of Confucius and
Yanzi in the context of poverty in the two *Analects* passages, however, is particularly effective, as one can see more clearly what this
Confucian joy consists of, since poverty is obviously not something
that by itself can bring joy to anyone.

In the later Confucian tradition, in addition to the *kong yan
zhi le*, there is also a joy in *cheng* 誠, than which Mencius claims
that there is no greater joy (*le mo da yan* 樂莫大焉): "Ten thousand
things are all here in me. There is no greater joy than finding that I
have realized myself through self-reflection (*fan shen er cheng* 反身
而誠)" (*Mencius* 7a4). Here I translate the Chinese word *cheng* 誠 as
"realization," in its double meanings in English. On the one hand,
through self-examination, one realizes (knows) oneself or, rather,
the nature (*xing* 性) or Dao within oneself; on the other hand, one
realizes (fulfils or completes) one's self-nature by being moral. It
is in this sense that Mencius says that there is no joy greater than
realization of oneself. If one feels joy for anything that is beneficial
to oneself, then certainly there cannot be any joy that is greater
than the joy in realizing oneself in the above-mentioned double
senses, since one certainly cannot do anything more beneficial to
oneself than to realize (know and fulfill) one's own nature. Yet this
realization, *cheng*, brings one the greatest joy, for a related reason: "the superior persons follow their nature, that is, humanity,
rightness, propriety, and wisdom, which are rooted in their heart–
mind. Its sleek appearance is inevitably manifested in their face
and backs and extended to their four limbs, rendering itself understood without words being used" (*Mencius* 7a21). The nature one
realizes in oneself is nothing but the four cardinal virtues, and as
soon as these virtues are fully realized, one will naturally, spontaneously, and joyfully practice from these virtues. So *cheng* is not
only self-regarding but also other-regarding. It is in this sense that
the *Doctrine of Mean* combines the two meanings of *cheng*, self-
realization and realization of others: "*cheng* is not only the realization of oneself but also the realization of others. Realization of the

self means humanity. Realization of other things means wisdom. These are the characters of the nature, and they are the Dao in which the internal and the external are united" (*Zhongyong* 25).

3. Being virtuous as being distinctively human

The significance of Confucius's emphasis on loving virtue as one loves sex can be better appreciated as a plausible answer to the question, "Why should I (or ought I to) be virtuous or moral?"—a question raised but never adequately answered in the Western philosophical tradition. In Plato's *Republic*, Glaucon asks the question "why should I be just?" and sharpens it with the famous Gyges's ring, which can make a person visible or invisible at will. Suppose that there are two such rings, with one for a just person and one for an unjust person. On the one hand, the unjust person uses the ring to make himself invisible when doing unjust things and visible when doing (or pretending to do) just things or at least not doing unjust things. In Glaucon's example, the unjust person is not someone who consistently does unjust things or does nothing but unjust things but someone who commits the greatest wrongs and yet secures for himself or herself a reputation for being just (Plato: 361a–b). On the other hand, the just person may use the ring to turn himself/herself invisible when doing just things and visible when not doing just things, and so "though doing no wrong he must have the repute of the greatest injustice" (Plato: 361c). In short, if an unjust person can have the appearance of being just or at least no appearance of being unjust, and a just person may have the appearance of being unjust or at least no appearance of being just, it may be asked: why should I be just? Here, as Glaucon's brother, Adimantus, points out, it seems that injustice pays much better than justice: "the consequences of my being just are, unless I likewise seem so, not assets, they say, but liabilities, labor, and total loss, but if I am unjust and have procured myself a reputation for justice, a godlike life is promised" (Plato: 365b).

This is perhaps the origin of the question "why be moral" that has troubled moral philosophers ever since. The question is puzzling, because it does not ask "why should *we* be moral?" which is relatively easy to answer: if we are not moral to each other, we will be living in Thomas Hobbes's state of nature, in which everyone is at war against everyone else, which benefits no one and hurts everyone. The question rather asks "why should *I* be moral?" Put more blatantly, it asks "why should I be moral to others, if my not being moral to them will not cause others to be equally not moral to me?" Obviously, this is a question raised by an egoist who is first of all concerned with his/her self-interest. To such a question, we might be tempted to answer: if everyone else acts immorally to others, thinking that his/her acting immorally will not cause others to be equally immoral to him/her, then everyone will act immorally to you; so you should be moral to others. However, such an answer is obviously not convincing to the person who poses the question: even if this were the case, since at least my being moral to others cannot guarantee that others will be moral to me, why should I be moral to them? It would certainly be much worse to me if I am moral to others while they are not moral to me.

Understood this way, the question "why be moral" has often been regarded as absurd, something we can simply ignore. Stephen Toulmin, for example, thinks that this question reaches "the limits of ethical reasoning—that is, the kind of occasion on which questions and considerations of an ethical kind can no longer arise" (Toulmin: 160). In his view, "ethical reasoning may be able to show why we ought to do this action as opposed to that, or advocate this social practice as opposed to that," but "there is no room *within* ethics for" the question "why ought one to do what is right"; to be moral is to do what I should do and to ask "why should I be moral" is to ask "why should I do what I should do," and this question, therefore, is "on a level with the question, 'Why are all scarlet things red?'" (Toulmin: 162). In other words, for Toulmin, the question "why should I be moral," just like the question "why are all scarlet things red," is a tautological question. To answer this question, we can only ask a rhetorical question, "What else 'ought' one to do?" (Toulmin: 162), just as to answer the question "why are scarlet things red?" we can only ask a rhetorical question: "what else can scarlet things be?"

While Toulmin regards this question as illegitimate because it is tautological, F. H. Bradley considers it unreasonable because it is self-contradictory: morality asks us to not be self-interested, but the person who asks the question "why should I be moral" is apparently looking for some self-interested reasons for being not self-interested. In his view, when we ask and attempt to answer the question of why be moral, we are regarding morality as a means to some further end, but morality is the end of itself, and so the question is unreasonable. He argues that "to take virtue as a mere means to an ulterior end is in direct antagonism to the voice of the moral consciousness. That consciousness, when unwarped by selfishness and not blinded by sophistry, is convinced that to ask for the Why? is simply immorality; to do good for its own sake is virtue, to do it for some ulterior end or object, not itself good, is never virtue; and never to act but for the sake of an end, other than doing well and right, is the mark of vice" (Bradley: 61–2).

Is then the question "why should I be moral" indeed as unreasonable as Toulmin and Bradley, among others, think? Morality tells one what he or she should do. When we ask people to be moral, we are essentially saying that "you should be moral"; in other words, we are saying that "you should be or do what you should be or do." So when someone asks the question "why should I be moral," the person is indeed asking "why should I be what I should be?" However, this is not a tautological question. Kai Nielsen makes an important distinction between the moral and nonmoral uses of the word "should." In the question "why should I be what I should be?" while the second "should" is indeed used in the moral sense, the first is used in a nonmoral sense. Thus, Nielsen points out:

> When I ask, "Why should I be moral?" I am not asking . . . "What moral reason or reasons have I for being moral?" That indeed is like asking "Why are all scarlet things red?" Rather I am asking, can I, everything considered, give a reason sufficiently strong—a non-moral reason clearly—for my always giving an overriding weight to moral considerations, when they conflict with other considerations, such that I could be shown to be acting irrationally, or at least less rationally than I otherwise would be acting, if I did not give such pride of place to moral considerations. (Nielsen 1989: 286–7)

In other words, the question "why should I be moral" asks "whether it is rational for me to be moral," assuming it is good for me to be moral. So the question is not tautological. However, if this is the case, does this mean that the question "why should I be moral" becomes a self-contradictory question, requesting a self-interested reason for being moral (not self-interested)? In appearance it is, as Bradley argues. David Copp, however, disagrees. In his view, to ask "what self-interested reasons do I have to be moral (to be not self-interested)" is to ask "does morality override self-interest? Or does self-interest override morality?" (see Copp: 86).

I agree with Nielsen and Copp that the question "why should I be moral" is neither tautological nor self-contradictory. It is a legitimate question. Given the simple fact that whoever asks the question does not have the inclination to be moral, it is crucial to make a distinction between moral justification and moral motivation. In its extended form, "why should I be what I should be?" the first "should" is not intended to provide a justification for the second "should." Otherwise, the morality would become something merely instrumental. Instead, the question "why should I be moral" or the first "should" in its extended form, "why should I be what I should be?" really concerns the issue of moral motivation. The person who asks the question is not a moral skeptic. He or she knows clearly that he or she should be moral but lacks the motivation to be so. A person who is motivated to be moral will never ask the question "why should I be moral?" Understood this way, the question really asks "what motivation(s) do or can I have to be moral?" and this seems to me a perfectly legitimate question.

There has never been a shortage of answers to this question in the Western philosophical tradition. In another place, I examined some representative ones and found them all wanting (see Huang 2008: 322–30). Here I shall argue that Confucius's view of loving virtue as one loves sex provides a most plausible answer to this question. From our discussion in the previous section, we can see that the Confucian answer to the question "why be moral" is that it is a joy to be moral; in other words, being moral is what pleases one's heart–mind, just like delicious food pleases one's mouth. Since one is naturally motivated to do things that please him or her, one should have the motivation to be moral. This answer may seem a little too simplistic: if so, the question "why be moral," which is really concerned about the motivation for morality, would not be raised in the first place, as everyone would already be motivated to be moral. Confucius's response is that, while people are naturally motivated to do what is joyful, they fail to distinguish two different kinds of joy and make a proper ranking between them.

Although the "joy of Confucius and Yanzi" (*kong yan zhi le*) is typically described as a joy one can still feel in poverty, Confucianism does not advocate asceticism and is therefore not opposing seeking joy in nonmoral things. Confucius says that "riches and honor are what every person desires" (*Analects* 4.5). In the *Analects*, there is also a famous passage, in which Confucius asks his students about their ambitions. After some have expressed their aspirations to administer a big invaded state, endowing its people with courage and correct principle, to rule a small state, making its people sufficient in their livelihood, to be a junior assistant, serving at ancestral temples and conferences of feudal lords, Zeng Dian 曾點, playing the zither, expresses his ideal: "in the late Spring, wearing the Spring dress, I would go with five or six grown-ups and six or seven children to bathe in the Yi River, enjoying the breeze from the Rain Dance Altar, and then returning home singing." After listening to them all, Confucius says, somewhat surprisingly, that "I agree with Zeng Dian (*wu yu dian ye* 吾與點也)" (*Analects* 11.26). Later Confucians have since all taken delight in talking about Confucius's "*wu yu dian ye.*"

The problem occurs only when one's seeking joy in nonmoral things leads to the violation of morality, or when one's seeking joy in being moral frustrates one's desires for nonmoral things. As we have seen, in such situations, Confucius clearly prizes the joy in being moral over joy in nonmoral things (*Analects* 4.5). This view is further developed by Mencius, according to whom, even when one seeks nonmoral joys in eating and drinking, one should regard it as providing a condition for one to seek moral joys; after all, one cannot do moral things when one lacks the physical strength to do so. Thus, Mencius claims that, "A person who cares only about food and drink is despised by others because the person takes care of the parts of less importance to the detriment of the parts of greater importance. However, if one can care about food and drink without neglecting any other part of his or her person, then his or her mouth and belly are more than just a foot or an inch of his or her skin" (*Mencius* 6a14). Mencius even claims that one should love morality more than life and hate immorality more than death.

Confucius himself makes it clear that to perform moral action often requires one to endure certain physical pains and even to sacrifice one's life: "People of knowledge and humanity may accept death in order to realize humanity but will not seek life at the price of humanity" (*Analects* 15.9). To live in poverty and sacrifice one's life of course causes pain. However, in Confucius's view, it causes one more pain to avoid pain and death by being immoral; to be rich and have a long life of course brings one joy; however, in Confucius's view, it brings one greater joy to be moral even if this excludes one from being rich and living a long life. It is in this sense that Confucius makes a distinction between beneficial joys and harmful joys: "Joy in being in accord with propriety and music, joy in praising the goodness of others, and joy in having good people as friends are beneficial joys. Joy in showing off, joy in living a dissolute life, and joy in being licentious are harmful joys" (*Analects* 16.5). In a similar vein, Mencius also talks about the three joys of superior persons: "The first joy is that parents are alive and brothers are well; the second joy is not being ashamed in face of heaven above and of other people under heaven; and the third joy is to have the most talented students in the empire" (*Mencius* 7a20). What is important is not the actual items regarded here as beneficial joys and joys of superior persons but the fact that the joy brought about by being moral is regarded as genuine joy, which should trump joys brought about by nonmoral and even immoral actions.

With this Confucian answer, the egoist who seeks joy and yet lacks the motivation for being moral, instead of asking "why should I be moral?" may ask "why should I seek moral joy rather than immoral joy?" After all, even though Confucius weighs moral joy more than immoral joy, the egoist certainly has a different assessment of the respective values of these two kinds of joy. To such an egoist, the Confucian answer is surprisingly simple: to be moral is characteristic of being human. This is related to the discussion of what is called "the distinction between humans and beasts" (*ren qin zhi bian* 人禽之辨), which continues throughout the history of Chinese philosophy. As we discussed in the previous chapter, when distinguishing human beings from beasts, instead of focusing on rationality as is common in the Western philosophical tradition, Confucius emphasizes the moral nature of human beings so much that anyone who is not moral is not regarded as a genuine or nondefective human being. While one may also find joy in doing nonmoral and/or immoral things, to be moral is a distinguishing mark of being human. So to be moral is a precondition for being a healthy or nondefective human being. This is most unique in the Confucian answer and is in sharp contrast to the conception of the human as rational, dominant in the Western philosophical tradition.[1]

So, ultimately, Confucius's answer to the question "why should I be moral?" is this: because you are a human being. Everyone has the motivation for joy. It is true that the joy can be sought either by following or violating moral principle. However, since the distinctive mark of being human is a moral heart–mind, and human beings are essentially moral beings, one should seek joy in being moral more than any other joy. I think this is a convincing answer, even to the egoist who raises the question. Of course, even if this is the case, it is very likely that the egoist is still not motivated to be moral. However, from the Confucian point of view, this betrays the stupidity or nearsightedness of the egoist, which contradicts what the egoist appears to be or thinks he or she is. The egoist normally appears to be, and indeed thinks he or she is, smarter than others. He or she may even laugh at people who perform moral actions, thinking that they are stupid, particularly if they do not try to let everyone else under heaven know that they are performing such moral actions; he or she can benefit himself or herself much more by performing immoral actions, particularly because he or she is smart enough to make himself or herself invisible when performing such immoral actions. From Confucius's point of view, however, it is the egoist who is stupid or near-sighted, to say the least, because they fail to recognize what is uniquely human in them.[2]

Because of such stupidity or near-sightedness, an immoral person does not know that, when seeking joy in doing immoral things, he or she is actually causing great harm to himself or herself, just like a person who takes good care of his or her tree but forgets to cure the disease of his own body, a person who takes care of his or her finger to the detriment of his or her shoulder and back, or a person who cares to look for his or her lost chickens and dogs but does not look for his or her own lost heart–mind. For this reason, an immoral person, again because of his or her stupidity, "dwells happily among dangers, looks upon disaster as profitable, and delights in what will lead them to perdition" (*Mencius* 4a8). An immoral person likes to have joy but causes the greatest harm to himself or herself as a human being without realizing it. It is in this sense that

Mencius says that the immoral person who "hates death and yet takes delight in being inhumane (*bur en* 不仁) is like one who hates drunkenness and yet drinks excessively" (*Mencius* 4a3).

4. Is a virtuous person foundationally egoistic or self-centered?

Our discussion above of Confucius's view on loving virtue as one loves sex gives rise to at least two questions. The first is whether Confucius's virtuous person is foundationally self-centered; the second is about the so-called paradox of virtue. I shall examine the first question in this section and the second question in the next section.

In appearance, it is silly to ask whether Confucius's virtuous person is self-centered or egoistic. As we have seen, clearly, just like Aristotle's virtuous person, Confucius's virtuous person is not egoistic or self-centered in the common sense, because such a person, precisely because of being virtuous, is concerned about the interest and welfare of others. Moreover, as we have shown in the previous chapter, Confucius's virtuous person, unlike Aristotle's genuine self-lover, is not egoistic or self-centered in a deeper sense: such a person is not only concerned with other people's external well-being but also with their internal well-being; in other words, they are not only interested in making themselves virtuous but also in making others virtuous.

However, there is a question about whether Confucius's virtuous person is *foundationally* self-centered or egoistic in the sense Thomas Hurka uses it. Hurka agrees with Aristotle, and so with Confucius, that a virtuous person is concerned with the interest of others; he would also further agree with Confucius that the interest of others a virtuous person is concerned with includes their characters; and he would even agree that the virtuous person is concerned with the good, both external and internal, of others for their sake and not merely for the sake of the agent himself or herself. However, Hurka claims that such a virtuous person is still self-centered or egoistic, for the virtuous person is concerned with the interest of others, including their characters, for their sake, ultimately because the person is concerned with his or her own interest in fully realizing his or her virtue. In Hurka's view, a virtuous "person's reasons for action derive from his flourishing," and so such a person is foundationally egoistic, insisting that his or her reasons to act and be motivated derive ultimately from his or her own flourishing (Hurka 2001: 232).

In appearance, Confucius's virtuous person is indeed an egoist in this sense. As we have seen, Confucius's answer to the question of "why be moral" is that you are a human being: to be moral is to be a healthy and nondefective human being. Although in order to be a healthy and nondefective human being, that is, a virtuous person, one need take care of other people's external interest and internal character, one does so still for the sake of one's own being a genuine and nondefective human being. After all, as an admirer of the golden age of the past, Confucius laments that "while the learners of the ancient are for the sake of themselves (*weiji* 為己), present learners are for the sake of others (*weiren* 為人)" (*Analects* 14.24).

Before we begin to answer whether Confucius's virtuous person is foundationally egoistic, therefore, it is important to understand what Confucius means by "for the sake of oneself" and "for the sake of others." When Confucius praises "the learners of the past" for their being for themselves, he means that they learn in order to cultivate themselves; while Confucius looks down upon the "present learners" for their being for others, he means that they learn only in order to decorate themselves with fine scholarship to impress others. To cultivate oneself (to be for the sake of oneself), in this Confucian tradition, means to become fully human by developing one's inborn tendencies to be concerned with others' interests, both internal and external. Therefore, the more one is for the sake of oneself, the more one is for the sake of others. In contrast, to show off one's scholarship in front of others (to be for the sake of others) is to be concerned with one's own interest (of fame). So the more one is for the sake of others in this sense, the more one is for the sake of oneself. Thus, commenting on this *Analects* passage, the neo-Confucian Cheng Yi 程頤 makes an interesting claim: "'The ancient learner is for the sake of oneself,' and the result is the fulfillment of others; 'the present learner is for the sake of others,' and the result is the loss of one's self" (Cheng and Cheng 1989: 325).

One way to respond to Hurka's claim that a virtuous person is still self-centered is that the virtuous person is foundationally or ultimately other-regarding. It is true that the virtuous person seeks his or her goal, but the goal he or she sets for himself or herself is to respect and further the good of others. In this sense, a virtuous person acts for his or her own sake only in the sense that he seeks to realize his own goal, which is to respect and further the good of others. In other words, a virtuous person is concerned with the good of others. Only in the sense that the goal of respecting and furthering the good of others is his or her own goal and not anyone else's goal can the virtuous person be regarded as being virtuous for his own sake. In this sense, the virtuous person is essentially foundationally other-regarding. Thus, if Hurka's objection claims that virtue ethics reduces the good of others to the good of the agent, this reply to the objection seems to claim that the good of the virtuous agent is reduced to that of others.

However, in this sense, Hurka claims that, instead of self-indulgence, a virtuous person now turns to be self-effacing: "to flourish or express virtue, a person must act from genuinely virtuous motives, such as a desire for another's pleasure for its own sake. If she instead aims at her own flourishing or virtue, she does not act from the required motives and so does not achieve the flourishing or virtue that is her goal. This requires the theories to be what Parfit calls self-effacing, telling agents not to be motivated by or even to think of their claims about source of their reasons" (Hurka 2001: 246). This seems to Hurka ironic, because "some partisans of virtue ethics have been vocal critics of the self-effacingness of consequential theories . . . but their own theories have the same feature, if anything in a more disturbing way" (Hurka 2001: 246).

To avoid this dilemma between self-indulgence and self-effacingness, a correct understanding of the nature of virtues, particularly Confucian virtues, is not to see them as either foundationally self-indulgent (for the sake of oneself by acting for the sake of others) or as foundationally self-effacing (for the sake of others through acting for one's own sake); it is rather to see it as both "to benefit others and to benefit oneself." Moreover, it is not to see them as two independent reasons, as if a virtuous person can have one without having the other or can have one before the other; it is rather to see them as two sides of one and the same reason. As we have seen, Confucius's virtuous person cannot be an altruist (serving the interests of others) without taking good care of one's own great body, to use Mencius' terms, which is his or her heart–mind.

In this sense, an altruist has to be an "egoist"; however, one cannot be an "egoist" (taking care of one's own great body) without serving the interests of others. In this sense, an "egoist" has to be an altruist. If asked why you act altruistically, the virtuous person will naturally reply that it is because he or she wants to be an altruistic person. It would then be very odd if Hurka wanted to claim that such a person is still foundationally egoistic: the person acts altruistically/selflessly only because the person wants to be an altruistic/selfless person and not because he or she really wants to act altruistically/selflessly. It is odd because obviously we cannot claim that a person acts really altruistically only when he or she does not want to be an altruistic person. In other words, it is odd because we cannot claim that an altruistic person is an egoist even in Hurka's foundational sense. At the same time, however, we cannot say such a person is self-effacing because it is the kind of person he or she wants to be, he or she is happy in being such a person, and he or she finds his or her true self in being such a person.

Thus, the two apparently antithetical ideas, egoism and altruism, the self-regarding and the other-regarding, or the self-indulgent and self-effacing, are combined. Moreover, they are combined not in such a way that a virtuous person is partially egoistic and partially altruistic or sometimes completely egoistic and sometimes completely altruistic, but in a way that the person is completely "egoistic" and completely "altruistic" simultaneously: a virtuous person acts entirely for the sake of one's true self and so is completely egoistic; however, this is only because the virtuous person defines his or her true self as one concerned with the good of others and so is entirely altruistic. It is not correct to say that the virtuous person is primarily or foundationally an "egoist" as if he or she takes care of the interests of others only as a means to serve the interest of his or her own true self, just as it is not correct to say that the virtuous person is primarily or foundationally an altruist as if he or she takes care of his or her own true self only as a way to serve others. Rather, altruism and egoism here completely overlap. As illustrated by the figure below used by Wittgenstein in his *Philosophical Investigations*, which looks like a duck in one way and a rabbit in another way, a virtuous person looks like an egoist in one way (he or she serves his or her own goal: being an altruist) and an altruist in another way (he or she sets his very goal to serve the interest of others). However, in Wittgenstein's figure, take away the rabbit, and you will not have the duck, and vice versa.

Similarly, in a virtuous person, take away egoism, and you will not have altruism left, and vice versa.

In this sense, it is wrong to ask whether a virtuous person does a virtuous thing because he or she thinks it is to his or her interest or because the person thinks it is a right thing to do. In the Kantian view, if the former, the person does the virtuous thing for a wrong reason; and only if the latter can the person's action have any genuine moral worth. In Confucius's view, however, to be self-interested and to be concerned with others are not only not contradictory; they are even not two things that happen to coincide perfectly: they are actually one and the same thing. When one seeks one's true self-interest, one must be performing moral actions; and when one performs moral actions, one must be seeking one's true self-interest. In this sense, it is even wrong to claim, as some do,[3] that one should first cultivate oneself (fulfilling one's own nature) and only later can one be concerned with the interest of others. One's true self-nature cannot be fulfilled without being concerned with the interest of others. Thus, we can say that a person seeks the interest of others (to be other-regarding) precisely in order to seek one's own interest (to be self-regarding); and we can also say that a person seeks one's own interest (to be self-regarding) precisely in order to serve the interest of others (to be other-regarding).

To be self-interested in this sense is identical to serving the interest of others. The very action that promotes the interest of others, precisely when and because it promotes the interest of others, promotes one's self-interest, as one's self-interest is precisely to promote the interest of others. Thus, the more virtuous (more concerned with the interest of others) a person is, the better his or her self-interest is served, and vice versa. So altruism and egoism, instead of being antithetical, come together as a unique conception of the ego or self. This ego or self that Confucius asks us to cultivate is the great ego or self, which is in contrast to the small ego or self, the ego or self in the familiar types of egoism. In Confucius's view, one can fully develop one's great ego or self only by overcoming one's small ego or self. This explains why, while advocating learning for the sake of one's self (the great self), Confucius also says that humanity, the most important Confucian virtue, can be realized only by overcoming one's self (the small self) (*Analects* 12.1).

5. A "dilemma of virtue"?

As we have seen, a truly virtuous person does virtuous things effortlessly, joyfully, and with great ease; however, virtues are praiseworthy precisely because they are supposed to be about things that are difficult for humans. This is what Philippa Foot calls the "dilemma of virtue" in her discussion of the Aristotelian virtue ethics. Foot argues that virtues are corrective with regard to humans' natural tendencies or, simply, human nature. What she means is that human beings either don't have a natural tendency to do what virtues require them to do or have a tendency to resist what virtues require them to do, and virtues are supposed to correct our natural tendencies in both cases. On the one hand, there are virtues that ask us to refrain from doing what we naturally tend to do. For example, there is "a virtue of industriousness only because idleness is a temptation; and of humility only because men tend to think too well of themselves" (Foot 1978: 9); on the other hand, there are virtues that require us to do what we do not have a natural tendency to do. For example, "if people were as much attached to the good of others as they are to their own good there would no more be a general virtue of benevolence than there is a general virtue of self-love. And if people cared about the rights of others as they care about their own rights no virtue of justice would be needed to look after the matter" (Foot 1978: 9). In Foot's view, both of these show that Aristotle is right that virtues are about what is difficult for humans.

However, since truly virtuous persons do not find any difficulty in doing what they are doing, that is, virtuous things, Foot detects a dilemma here: "we both are and are not inclined to think that the

harder a man finds it to act virtuously the more virtue he shows if he
does act well. For on the one hand great virtue is needed where it is
particularly hard to act virtuously; yet on the other it could be argued
that difficulty in acting virtuously shows that the agent is imperfect
in virtue: according to Aristotle, to take pleasure in virtuous action
is the mark of true virtue, with the self-mastery of the one who finds
virtue difficult only a second best" (Foot 1978: 10). Aristotle's view
mentioned here is precisely the same as Confucius's: a truly virtuous
person does virtuous things with joy and ease. However, Aristotle
also says that virtue is about what is difficult for humans, and precisely because they are about what is difficult for humans, we regard
virtuous actions as of higher moral worth. But it now turns out, par-
adoxically, that truly virtuously persons are doing virtuous things
without any difficulty; as a matter of fact, they do them, as we have
seen, effortlessly, joyfully, and with great ease.

Foot's own solution to this dilemma is to make a distinction
between human beings in general and virtuous persons in particular: "What is certain is that the thought that virtues are corrective
does not constrain us to relate virtue to difficulty in each individual man. Since men in general find it hard to face great dangers
or evils, and even small ones, we may count as courageous those
few who without blindness or indifference are nevertheless fearless
even in terrible circumstances. . . . I have argued that the virtues
can be seen as correctives in relation to human nature in general
but not that each virtue must present a difficulty to each and every
man" (Foot 1978: 11). In other words, even though virtuous persons do virtuous things without difficulty, their actions are still
praiseworthy, because they are doing what is difficult for humans
in general. This solution is not entirely satisfactory. Since virtue
is praiseworthy, precisely because it is about difficult things, but
since such things are not difficult for virtuous persons, why should
we also regard actions by such persons as praiseworthy? Only if
the same actions are performed by nonvirtuous persons, who perform them by exerting great effort (to resist their strong inclination
not to do so) could such actions be regarded as praiseworthy. Of
course, then it turns out that we are saying, oddly, that it is the
nonvirtuous persons' actions, not the virtuous persons' actions, if
they are performing the same actions, that are praiseworthy.

Confucius's solution to the apparent dilemma is different and, I
shall argue, more plausible. The upshot of this solution is not just
to look at the end-result of how a virtuous person and nonvirtuous

person perform a virtuous action (the former with ease, the latter with difficulty) but to look at the process through which a virtuous person becomes virtuous and the process through which a non-virtuous person becomes or remains nonvirtuous. When we pay attention to the end-result, it is indeed somewhat plausible to claim that a nonvirtuous person's action is more praiseworthy than a virtuous person's action, if both are doing the same thing, but the latter does it effortlessly, while the former does it by exerting great effort. However, Confucius's view is that we should not just look at the end-result; we should also look at the situation historically.

It is true that a virtuous person does virtuous things effortlessly, but it certainly takes him or her great effort to become a virtuous person; it is also true that a nonvirtuous person does the virtuous thing with great effort but this is precisely because the person has not taken great effort to become a virtuous person. The very fact that Confucius says "I have never seen a person who loves virtue as he loves sex" shows that, for Confucius, it is not something easy to love virtue as one loves sex. Moreover, although Confucius does not deny the possibility of persons born to be sages, persons who are born to love virtues as they love sex, as Cai Shangsi 蔡尚思 (1905–2008) points out: "Confucius himself does not really believe that there are indeed 'people who are born with knowledge,' for he not only laments that he has never seen a 'sage,' denies that he himself is a sage by birth, but also clearly denies that he himself is 'one born with knowledge'" (Cai 1982: 99). After all, Confucius himself could do things at his heart's desire without overstepping bounds only after he reached the age of 70.

How then can one become virtuous? Confucius's answer is that it is through learning. His seven-sentence autobiography lists the six landmarks in his moral self-cultivation. The last stage, as mentioned, is at age 70, when he can do things at his heart's desire. The first stage is at age 15, when he "sets his heart–mind on learning" (*Analects* 2.4). He claims that it is indeed his love for learning that separates himself from many others: "in a neighborhood of ten households, there must be those who are as diligent and trust-worthy as myself, but there is no one who loves to learn as much as I do" (*Analects* 5.28). In another place, he says that he dare not claim to be a sage or a person with the virtue of humanity; if there is anything special about himself, he says that "it is no more than the fact that I'm never tired of learning and never impatient in teaching" (*Analects* 7.34; see also *Analects* 7.2).

In this context, there is nothing wrong in acknowledging one's lack of knowledge, and one should "be eager and quick to learn and feel no shame in asking people of lower stations" (*Analects* 5.15). He says that "there are people who like to make up things without possessing knowledge, but I don't have this fault. I would like to use my ears broadly and follow what is good in things I hear" (*Analects* 7.28). One important way to learn is to learn from others. In one place, he says that "even when walking in the company of two other persons, I must be able to find my teachers: copy their good qualities and avoid their bad qualities" (*Analects* 7.22). In another place, he says something similar: "when seeing a person better than yourself, try to be his or her equal; when seeing a person worse than yourself, try to reflect upon yourself [about how not to become such a person]" (*Analects* 4.17).

The importance of learning is made most clear by Confucius in a passage in which he discusses six moral flaws, which are all caused by one's not paying attention to learning: "the flaw of loving [the virtue of] humanity without the love to learn is being foolish; the flaw of loving knowledge without the love to learn is to deviate from the right path; the flaw of loving trustworthiness without the love to learn is to lead to harmful behavior; the flaw of loving uprightness without the love to learn is to be intolerant; the flaw of loving courage without the love to learn is to be insubordinate; and the flaw of loving to have a strong will without the love to learn is being arrogant" (*Analects* 17.8). It is noteworthy that all six qualities are positive, but Confucius emphasizes that they become problematic when not accompanied by one's love for learning. One may wonder what the love to learn adds to or how it complements these good qualities.

If we look at the flaw of each of the six good qualities when not accompanied by the love to learn, we can see that the main function of learning is to make sure that the respective quality be manifested appropriately in different situations. For example, the most important feature of the virtue of humanity is to love people. If one's love for this virtue is not accompanied by the love for learning, one may love all people, virtuous or vicious, poor or rich, old or young, etc., in exactly the same way, which Confucius says is foolish. In Confucius's view, while one ought to love everyone, one's love for different people, in order to be appropriate, should be different, taking into consideration the uniqueness of each of one's objects of love. The function of learning in this case is to find the way of love that is appropriate to each unique object of love. For another example, trustworthiness, or to make good one's word, is a positive quality that Confucius also emphasizes a great deal. However, this does not mean that one ought to keep every word one says regardless of any particular situation. If I promised to play a game of chess with one of my friends, but on my way to my friend's house, I saw a child falling into a river, my action would be harmful if I single-mindedly decided to keep the promise I made to my friends without making the effort to save the child. So the function of learning here in relation to trustworthiness is to discern in every particular situation whether and how I should make good my words.

Generally speaking, thus, the six good qualities tell us what we should do in general, while the function of learning is to tell us how to manifest such good qualities appropriately in particular cases. In this sense, I think Li Zehou 李澤厚, a contemporary Chinese scholar, is right, in his comment on this *Analects* passage, that the function of learning is "to grasp the appropriate degree (or measure)" (Li Zehou 1999: 398). This is consistent with what Confucius says about learning in another place: "If one learns, one will not be inflexible" (*Analects* 1.8),[4] and inflexibility is one of the four things that Confucius warns us against, along with making groundless speculations, insisting on absolute certainty, and being egoistic (*Analects* 9.4).

The content of Confucius's learning is thus not bookish knowledge or technical skills but the way to become a virtuous person. This is made most clear in his praise of his most favorite student Yan Hui. Duke Ai of Lu asks Confucius which student of his loves learning. Confucius responds: "There was one Yan Hui who loved to learn, never shifting his proper anger to an unrelated person and never making the same mistake twice. Unfortunately, he died young. Now there is no one. I've not heard of anyone else who loves to learn that much" (*Analects* 6.3). Here, Confucius related the love to learn to Yan Hui's two prominent characters. Oftentimes when we are angry at someone, even with proper reasons, we cannot help but shift the anger to someone else who happens to come to our scene. And many times we continue to do wrong things even when they are pointed out to us. Confucius says that his student Yan Hui, who loves to learn, does not have either of the two faults. So learning in this particular case is crucial to Yan Hui's avoiding them. Thus, in his famous essay, "What Does Yanzi Love to

Learn?" the neo-Confucian in the Song dynasty Cheng Yi answers the title question: "it is to learn the way to be a sage." He further explains that the way to be a sage is to train one's emotion according to what is uniquely human, which is in contrast to what inferior people do: to let one's emotion dictate what a human being is (see Cheng and Cheng 1989: 577).

So Confucius uses the term "learning" in a sense that is different from its usual sense. Zixia, one of Confucius's students, makes an explicit distinction between the two in two sayings, also recorded in the *Analects*. In one place, Zixia says, "common people of trades practice in their workshops to master their respective skills, but superior persons learn to acquire *Dao*," the way to become sages (*Analects* 19.7). In another place, Zixia says, "If one judges one's wife in terms of character instead of beauty, if one serves one's parents with his whole heart, if one gives one's life in serving one's ruler, and if one deals with friends with trust, then this person must have learned even if the person says that he has not" (*Analects* 1.7). Here, we can imagine, the person may say that he or she has not learned because, in the usual sense, to learn is to read books and to listen to lectures to acquire theoretical knowledge or practical skills; and in this sense, the person may indeed have not learned, as it is entirely possible that this person may be illiterate. However, Zixia claims that this person must have learned because the content of learning here is how to become a virtuous person in dealing with various human relationships. Unless a person was born to be a sage, which Confucius says that he has never seen, one must learn to be a virtuous person.

This point is particularly important, because for Confucius to learn to be a virtuous person is something that everyone can do. Thus when one of his students, Ranqiu 冉求, says "it is not that I'm not pleased with your way; it is that my ability comes short," Confucius responds "a person whose ability comes short stops in the middle. However, you even have not started yet" (*Analects* 6.12). Indeed, Confucius says that he has never seen a person who lacks ability to practice virtue. What is important is, if one has not started, to get started and, if one has already started, as Confucius did when he was 15 years old, to never stop. Confucius says that this is just like making a mound. One should not stop until the last basketful of earth is completed. It is also like leveling ground.

One has started even by tipping just one basketful of earth (see *Analects* 9.19).[5] This point is further developed by Mencius. In the same passage in which he claims that there are things one desires more than life and there are things one hates more than death, Mencius argues that "not only worthy people have such a heart–mind; common people all have it. The worthy people simply make sure that it does not get lost" (*Mencius* 6a10). In this respect, Mencius argues that sages and the rest of us are of the same kind: "Things of the same kind are all alike. How can there be an exception when it comes to humans? Sages and I are of the same kind. Thus Longzi said that 'when someone makes a shoe for a foot he has not seen, I am sure that he will not produce a basket.' All shoes are alike because all feet are alike" (*Mencius* 6a7). Since sages and the rest of us are alike, if sages can find joy in being moral, then everyone can do it too. The reason is that everyone has a heart–mind, which a common thing must exist to please.

With such a historical understanding of the difference between a virtuous person and a nonvirtuous person when they are both doing virtuous things, Foot's dilemma of virtue disappears. Virtue now is about what is difficult not only to humans in general but also to virtuous persons. It involves things difficult for virtuous persons not in the sense that virtuous persons find it difficult to do, as they don't, but in the sense that it is difficult for anyone to become virtuous. Thus, a virtuous person's action is still praiseworthy, even though he or she performs this action joyfully, effortlessly, and with great ease. A similar action done by a nonvirtuous person is not equally admirable. Although the person is doing the thing that is difficult for him or her, as he or she has to exert great effort to do this virtuous thing by resisting his or her strong inclination not to do it or to do a vicious thing instead, the very reason that the person finds it difficult to do the virtuous thing is precisely that the person has not exerted great effort to become a virtuous person in the first place. In other words, if we understand that it is easy for one to be a nonvirtuous person, in the sense that one does not need to make efforts to cultivate oneself, and it is difficult for one to be a virtuous person, in the sense that one needs to make great effort to cultivate oneself, then virtue is indeed about what is difficult even to virtuous persons.

6. Conclusion

In the above, we have examined Confucius's view of loving virtue as one loves sex. In concluding this chapter, I want to show why it is not enough simply to do virtuous things; one also must love doing them. In other words, I want to show what moral value one's love for virtue adds to one's virtuous actions. To respond, first of all, we have to agree that the moral life recommended by virtue ethics must be a better life for the agent than the lives recommended by alternative theories of ethics. For example, Michael Stocker asks, "what sort of life would people live who did their duties but never or rarely wanted to?" (Stocker 1997: 67). Obviously, whether such a life is good for others to whom one performs moral duties, this cannot be a good life for the moral agent, as the agent has to make a great effort to overcome his or her natural inclination in order to perform moral actions and therefore cannot take delight in performing such actions. This is made most clear by Kant's separation of morality from happiness. Of course, critics of virtue ethics might think that whether a moral life is good to the agent is irrelevant; what matters is whether it is good for moral patients. However, contrary to what we may normally think, such moral actions are not good even for moral patients either. This point is made most clear by Michael Stocker's following hypothetical scenario:

> Suppose you are in a hospital, recovering from a long illness. You are very bored and restless and at loose ends when Smith comes in once again. You are now convinced more than ever that he is a fine fellow and a real friend—taking so much time to cheer you up, traveling all the way across town, and so on. You are so effusive with your praise and thanks that he protests that he always tries to do what he thinks is his duty, what he thinks will be best. . . . [T]he more you two speak, the more clear it becomes that . . . it is not essentially because of you that he came to see you, not because you are friends, but because he thought it his duty . . . or simply because he knows of no one more in need of cheering up and no one easier to cheer up. (Stocker 1997: 74)

This example shows clearly that only when and because a virtuous person's action benefiting others makes this virtuous person's life better can it make the life of others better.

CHAPTER FOUR

Moral education: How to teach what can only be learned by oneself

1. Introduction

Although the common perception of Confucius as the first private teacher in Chinese history may be wrong,[1] it is beyond doubt that his influence as a private teacher is unparalleled in Chinese history; and while it might be an exaggeration that Confucius had more than 3,000 students, it must be true that he had many. In this chapter, I shall first examine an apparent inconsistency in Confucius's view on whether everyone is perfectible through education (Section 2). To understand this apparent inconsistency, I shall argue that the education that Confucius had in mind is primarily moral education, as his goal was to help his students to become virtuous persons. This reflects the Socratic question about whether virtue can be taught (Section 3). I shall argue that, while Confucius's answer to the question is affirmative, he does not think that virtue can be taught in the same way as theoretical knowledge or technical skills are taught. For Confucius, the most effective way to teach people to be virtuous is by being a moral exemplary oneself (Section 4). As Confucius does not separate the personal and the political, a dogma in contemporary political liberalism, he argues that the primary function of government is moral education of its people, particularly not through laws and public policies but through the exemplary conduct of political rulers (Section 5). The chapter will conclude with a brief summary (Section 6).

2. An apparent paradox in Confucius's philosophy of education

Confucius makes the famous claim that "education should be provided to all without any group (*lei* 類) discrimination" (*Analects* 15.39). The significance of this claim is primarily not about equal opportunity of education but about the perfectibility of all: education will make a difference to a person whether the person is rich or poor, talented or not so talented, good or bad, and noble or base. This is revolutionary because both official schools and private schools before and during Confucius's time were primarily open only to nobles. While we do not have entirely reliable sources (see Hu 1998: 1.87–88), we do learn from *Shiji* 史記 (*Records of the History*), *Lü Shi Chuqiu* 呂氏春秋 (*Mister Lü's Springs and Autumns*), and other parts of the *Analects* itself that, among Confucius' students, Zilu 子路 was originally "uncultivated" (*ye ren* 野人), Zigong 子貢 was engaged in commerce (an occupation looked down upon), Zhonggong's 仲弓 father was a "lowly person" (*jian-ren* 賤人), Zizhang 子張 was from a family of low status in the state of Lu 魯, and Yan Zhuju 顏涿聚 was a robber (see Cai 1982: 192). In fact, among Confucius's students, very few are from rich and noble families. Moreover, of those mentioned here, Zilu, Zigong, and Zhonggong are among Confucius's ten most accomplished students (see *Analects* 11.3), and Confucius thinks that Zhonggong can even be the ruler of a state (see *Analects* 6.1). Xu Fuguan 徐復觀 (1904–82), a prominent contemporary Confucian, thus argues that one of the most important contributions that Confucius makes to Chinese culture is that he "breaks free of all unreasonable distinctions among human beings and advocates that all humans are of one class and are equal" (Xu 1999: 64).

Confucius' conviction that everyone is perfectible through education is to an extent based upon his metaphysical view of human nature: "human beings are alike in terms of their inborn nature but become different through practice" (*Analects* 17.2). As the topic of whether human nature is good or evil became a serious debate among later Confucians, scholars often try to figure out what his view on this issue is from this passage, the only one in the *Analects* in which he talks about human nature. It is clear that this passage alone cannot give us a clear answer. What it does tell us is that education makes all the difference. The trouble in our understanding of Confucius's view, however, is the immediate next passage, which in some versions of the *Analects* is combined with this current one as one single passage, in which Confucius says something that seems to be contradictory: "only the most stupid and the most wise cannot change" (*Analects* 17.3). A common explanation is that *Analects* 17.2 states a general rule, while *Analects* 17.3 is intended to provide an exception to it. Chen Daqi, for example, thinks that Confucius holds a view of human nature as three-graded: the wise above (very few), the stupid below (also very few), and the people in the middle (majority). So *Analects* 17.2 is about the majority in the middle, to whom education is important, while *Analects* 17.3 is about the two extremes, to whom education is either unnecessary or ineffective (Chen Daqi 1964: 277).[2]

To have a better understanding, we must look at a similar passage in the *Analects*. Seeing one of his students, Zai Yu, sleeping during the day, Confucius says, "a piece of rotten wood cannot be carved, nor can a wall of dried dung be trowelled. As far as Yu is concerned, what is the use of condemning him?" (*Analects* 5.10). Clearly, Zai Yu must belong to the most stupid who cannot be changed. If this were the case, Confucius would not waste time continuing to teach him. However, this was not the case. Zai Yu not only remained his student but became one of the ten with the highest achievements. Confucius compares Zai Yu with a piece of rotten wood that cannot be carved and a wall of dried dung that cannot be trowelled because Zai Yu sleeps during the day. In other words, he does not make an effort to learn and therefore belongs to those who do not study even when vexed with difficulties.[3] Thus when Confucius says that stupid people cannot change, he really means that those who do not learn will not become wise. As long as one is willing to learn, anyone can become wise.

Thus, Confucius says that he has never seen anyone who lacks the necessary intellectual ability to learn (*Analects* 4.6). When one of his students, Ran Qiu, says that "it is not that I am not pleased with your way, but my ability is lacking," Confucius says that "those who say their abilities are lacking are really people who give up on themselves along the way. In your case, you set a limit for your-self beforehand" (*Analects* 6.12). So Confucius asks his students to never give up in the middle with the excuse of having insufficient abilities. In this view, to learn "can be compared with making a mound: if the mound is short of one last basketful of soil, it is because I stopped; it can also be compared with leveling the ground: if the last basketful of soil is also gone, it is because I continue to make the progress" (*Analects* 9.19). It is in this sense that I think Song Dynasty neo-Confucian Cheng Yi's following interpretation of the passage in question, *Analects* 17.3, radical in appearance, grasps what Confucius means: Confucius "does not mean that peo-ple cannot be changed. It means that there is a principle that cannot be changed. Only two kinds of people cannot be changed: those who lack self-confidence and those who abandon themselves. They are unwilling to learn. If they are willing to learn, have confidence in themselves, and do not give up on themselves, how can they not change themselves?" (Cheng and Cheng 1989: *Yishu* 19; 252; see Huang 2009). What Cheng Yi means by the principle that cannot be changed is this: anyone who gives up on himself or herself will not become wise, and anyone who exerts effort can become wise.

If our understanding above is correct, however, *Analects* 8.9 becomes a really puzzling passage: "common people can/may (*ke* 可) be made to do things but can/may not (*bu ke* 不可) be made to know things." Since the word *ke* can mean either "can" or "may (are permitted to)" and its negative *bu ke* can correspondingly mean either "cannot" or "may not (are not permitted to)," tradi-tionally, there have been two main interpretations of this passage. According to one interpretation, the word *ke* means "be permitted to" so that Confucius was understood to be saying that common people are permitted to be made to do things but are not permitted to be made to understand them. Not only critics of Confucius and Confucianism, particularly during the Communists' Anti-Confucius campaign in the 1970s, adopted this interpretation to show that Confucius wanted to keep the common people in ignorance, it was also adopted by more sympathetic commentators. For example, the Qing dynasty scholar Yan Xizhai 顏習齋 (1635–1704) not only defended this interpretation but also argued against the alterna-tive interpretation of the word *ke* to mean *neng* 能 (can). In his view, if people are made to know things, "their ears and eyes will be deluded and their heart/mind will be misled. That is why it is not permitted to be made known to people. With this sagely learning getting lost, later Confucians have claimed that what is meant here is that people cannot be made to know things and not that they are not permitted to know things. For this reason, everyone tries to invent ways to make people to know things; the result is that both scholarship and the way of government are destroyed" (in Cheng Shude 1990: 533).

According to the other traditional interpretation, which has now been accepted by most contemporary scholars, the word *ke* should be understood as "can" so that what Confucius says is that "common people can be made to do things but cannot be made to know things." The crucial question then is why people cannot be made to know certain things. The typical answer is that common people lack the intellectual ability to know things. For example, the Han 漢 dynasty scholar Zheng Xuan 鄭玄 (127–200) holds that the word here translated as "common people," *min* 民, really means "stupid people," *ming* 冥, who are at a remove from the way of humanity (in Cheng Shude: 532). Although not regarding people to be at a remove from humanity, the Qing Dynasty scholar Zhao You 趙佑 also noted that common people are stupid: "The nature of common people is originally stupid and so they cannot be made to know things. Therefore, to maintain order, rulers should discuss things among themselves and establish rules for people to follow. If so, everything will be in order" (in Cheng Shude 1990: 533).

So according to one interpretation, Confucius advocates a policy of keeping common people in ignorance (*yumin* 愚民), while according to the other interpretation, Confucius laments the fact that common people are too stupid to know things (*minyu* 民愚). However, neither of these two interpretations seems plausible. The first interpretation cannot be right. As pointed out by Chen Daqi, "it is contrary to Confucius's thought. In two different places, [*Analects*] 9.19 and 14.28, Confucius says that the person who knows will not be deluded. On this principle, unless Confucius wished to keep people in delusion forever, he would not be unwilling to transform people from ignorance to knowledge" (Chen Daqi 1969: 153).[4] The second interpretation cannot be right, as it is directly contradictory to Confucius's view that we have been discussing so far in this section, that everyone is perfectible through education. To have a better understanding, we must know why Confucius thinks people cannot be made to know and why.

3. Confucius as a moral educator

What is the goal of Confucius's education and what kind of persons does Confucius want his students to become? To see these, we must know what Confucius taught. We can get some clues to the answer to this question from such things as "Four Subjects" (*si ke* 四科), "Four Teachings" (*si jiao* 四教), and "Six Classics" (*liu jing* 六經).

First, the "Four Subjects" are mentioned in the following passage in the *Analects*: "Virtuous conduct: Yan Yuan, Ming Ziqian, and Ran Boniu; Speech: Zai Wo and Zigong; Governmental affairs: Ran You and Ji Lu; and Literature: Ziyou and Zixia" (*Analects* 11.3). This is the famous list of what came to be known as the "Four Subjects with Ten Philosophers" (*sike shizhe* 四科十哲). From the "Biographies of Confucius' Disciples" of *Shiji* (*Records of History*) by Sima Qian, we know that Confucius had more than 3,000 students, among whom over 70 grasped the Six Classics (or Six Arts), to be discussed later in this section. Obviously, the 10 mentioned in this *Analects* passage are the most outstanding of the 70 students, particularly in terms of their respective achievements in the four subjects of Confucius's teaching. Although there is still controversy about the authorship of this *Analects* passage,[5] and it is unlikely that Confucius taught these four subjects in the same way as we teach, in today's university setting, such subjects as English, mathematics, physics, sociology, etc. (although in the Han Dynasty, it was according to these four subjects that officials were selected), it is nevertheless true that these four are the most important aspects of his teaching.

Looking at the Four Subjects, we see that the first, virtuous conduct, and the third, political affairs, or virtuous management of government, are clear examples of Confucius's moral teaching. The fourth one, literature, is commonly understood to refer to the six classics, textbooks used by Confucius in his moral education, as we will discuss in detail below. The only subject that causes some trouble is the second, speech, because there are numerous passages in the *Analects* in which Confucius looks down upon people who are good at speech. For example, when told that Yong, one of his students, has the virtue of humanity but unfortunately does not have a facile tongue, Confucius says that, although he does not know whether Yong indeed has the virtue of humanity, "what use is there for a facile tongue? A person who is quick in speaking can only offend people" (*Analects* 5.5). For this reason, Confucius says that "he dislikes eloquent people" (*Analects* 11.25). In his view, "anyone with flowery words and ingratiating face is hardly one of humanity (*ren* 仁)" (*Analects* 1.3; see also 5.25, 13.27, and 17.7); in contrast, "a superior person is slow in speaking" (*Analects* 12.3). So it is clear that those students who have high achievements in the subject of speech must be different from, for example, those students who earn good grades in speech courses today.

A number of related passages in the *Analects* make it clear that those students of Confucius who excel in the subject of speech must have two traits. The first is trustworthiness. Thus, Confucius says that a person's being "trustworthy in speech" can be regarded as a mark of being learned (*Analects* 1.7); "to be trustworthy is similar to being morally right (*yi* 義) in the sense of keeping a promise" (*Analects* 1.13); "either one does not speak or one speaks sincerely" (*Analects* 11.14); and "the ancient people were loathe to speak, because it was shameful if one failed to keep up with one's words" (*Analects* 4.22). The second is the priority of action to speech. Thus, Confucius says that a superior person "is quick in action but cautious in speech" (*Analects* 1.14), "puts words into action before allowing words to follow the action" (*Analects* 2.13), "is slow in speaking but quick in action" (*Analects* 4.24), "only says things that will be practiced" (*Analects* 13.3), "is ashamed of saying more and doing less" (*Analects* 14.27), and is "conscientious and trustworthy in word and single-minded and reverent in deed" (*Analects* 15.5). As both traits are moral traits, speech, like the three other subjects, is a subject of moral education.[6]

Second, regarding the "Four Teachings," the *Analects* records a student's report: "The master has four teachings: literature, action, loyalty, and trustworthiness" (*Analects* 7.25). The first item, referring to the six classics, will be discussed separately. The question is about the relationship among the other three items, action (*xing* 行), loyalty (*zhong* 忠), and trustworthiness (*xin* 信). Yuan dynasty scholar Chen Tianxiang 陳天祥, for example, argues that *xing* is a general term of virtuous action, while *zhong* and *xin* are two particular virtuous actions: "to be loyal and to be trustworthy are already virtuous actions, and to act virtuously already includes being loyal and trustworthy. It is difficult to understand why loyalty and trustworthiness have to be added to virtuous actions" (in Cheng Shude 1990: 486–7). So some scholars suspect that this passage in the *Analects* must be a mistake on the part of the student who reports it (see Chen Daqi 1964: 293–4; Li Zehou 1999: 184–5; Kuang Yaming 1990: 300, note 2). While it does not matter that much to the purpose of this essay, it is noteworthy that there has also been a long commentary history trying to make sense of it. The most sophisticated one is provided by the greatest neo-Confucian synthesizer, Zhu Xi 朱熹, who tries to show that these four items actually represent a gradual process of moral education from the easiest to the most difficult (see Cheng Shude 1990: 487). However, I think the Jin dynasty scholar Li Chong's 李充 interpretation makes the best sense. According to Li, since loyalty is a virtuous action in relation to one's superiors, and trustworthiness is a virtuous action in relation to one's friends, *xing* must be understood in a narrow sense of virtuous action within one's family (see Cheng Shude: 486). In any case, however one understands the precise meanings of these three teachings, it is clear that the emphasis of Confucius's teaching is on virtue.

Third, the "Six Classics," which, as we have seen above, is listed as one of the "Four Subjects," *wenxue*, and one of the "Four Teachings," *wen*, refers to the textbooks Confucius used to teach his students. Such texts were used in official schools prior to Confucius. However, by Confucius's time, they became fragmentary, mixed, and repetitive (with multiple versions). It is not clear about his precise role in the formation of what came to be known as Six Classics: the *Book of Poetry,* the *Book of Documents*, the *Book of Rites,* the *Book of Music*, the *Book of Change*, and the *Spring and Autumn Annals.* Some claim that they were all formed after Confucius, while others claim that Confucius wrote them (see Kuang Yaming 1990: 341). It is more plausible that Confucius edited these texts, although the five classics as handed down today (the sixth, the *Book of Music*, is unfortunately no longer extant) were edited in the Han Dynasty and so are not exactly the same ones as Confucius used.

There is a widespread opinion that, among the four teachings and the four subjects, while three are clearly for moral education, the subject of *wenxue* or the teaching of *wen*, the six classics, is to provide the student with intellectual knowledge (see for example Kuang Yaming 1990: 303–7; Cai Shangsi 1982: 197). I think this is a misunderstanding. When Confucius teaches the six classics, he does not do so as a professor of classics does today: to provide curious students with knowledge of ancient texts. Instead, Confucius uses these six classics as a vehicle of moral education. For example, regarding the function of these six classics, Confucius says,

> When you enter a state, you can see how its people are cultivated. If you see them behaving warmly and honestly, you know that they are cultivated by the *Book of Poetry*; if you see them being perceptive of current affairs and conscious of historical events, you know that they are cultivated by the *Book of Documents*; if you see them broad-minded, easy-going, and kind, you know that they are cultivated by the *Book of Music*; if you see them pure, calm, and careful, you know that they are cultivated by the *Book of Change*; if you see them modest, frugal, serious, and reverent, you know that they are cultivated by the *Book of Rites*; and if you see them good at making judgment of events from a historical perspective without distortion, you know that they are cultivated by the *Spring and Autumn Annals*. (*Liji* 26.1)

It is clear that, for Confucius, we study classics not simply to satisfy our curiosity about what ancient people thought but to become better persons ourselves.

Among these six classics, those Confucius talks about most, as recorded in the *Analects*, are *Poetry*, *Rites*, and *Music*. The significance of these three in moral education is best summarized in *Analects* 8.8: "arising from the *Poetry*, established by the *Rites*, and accomplished by the *Music*." As in many cases in classical Chinese, the subject of these three sentences is not mentioned. However it is commonly believed to be virtue or a virtuous person, and so the passage says something to the effect that a person is initiated into virtue through poetry, his or her virtuous conduct is stabilized by rites, and he and she becomes effortless in being virtuous through music. It is clear that, for Confucius, moral education is not to issue moral commands but to stimulate a person's moral sentiments. For this purpose, Confucius thinks that the poems included in the *Book of Poetry* are most effective. Thus, he asks his students to study these poems, which "can serve to stimulate one's imagination, sharpen one's sensitivity, increase one's sense of solidarity, and improve one's way to handle complaints [about immoral things]. Near, one can learn how to serve one's parents; far, one can learn how to serve one's lord" (*Analects* 17.9). This is because, for Confucius, "the three hundred poems in the book can be summarized in one sentence: do not think of diverting from the right path" (*Analects* 2.2). Confucius's interest in the function of the moral dimension of the poetry is also clear in his disapproval of other ways of reading them: "If one reads these three hundred poems and yet fails [to put them into practice] when assuming a governmental position and is unable to handle things on a mission to foreign states, then it is useless, however many times you have read them" (*Analects* 13.5).

However, one's moral sentiments stimulated by poetry are momentary and not stable. For example, in contemporary society, our moral sentiments may arise by watching a movie, reading a newspaper report, or seeing a scene of natural disaster on television. However, after leaving the movie theater, putting down the newspaper, or turning off the television, such moral sentiments may soon be gone. In order to stabilize the moral sentiments initiated by poetry, Confucius stresses the importance of rules of propriety: "being respectful without propriety, one will feel tired; being cautious without propriety, one will become timid; being courageous without propriety, one will become unruly, and being upright without propriety, one will become intolerant" (*Analects* 8.2). So he asks his students "not to look at, listen to, speak, or do things against rules of propriety" (*Analects* 12.1). Rules of propriety are not like punitive laws. In violating rules of propriety, one is not to be punished but will feel ashamed as one will be looked down upon in the community. Still, in performing moral conduct stabilized by rules of propriety, one will feel some uneasiness and often need to exert effort to overcome one's desire to look at, listen to, speak, or do things against rules of propriety. Thus Confucius thinks that moral education has to be accomplished in music.

As we mentioned, the *Book of Music* is now lost, but there is a chapter on music in the existing version of the *Book of Rites*, from which we can learn in what sense morality is accomplished in music. The Chinese word for music, *yue* 樂, when pronounced differently, also means joy or delight or happiness, *le* 樂. Thus the *Book of Rites* says that "music (*yue* 樂) is joy (*le* 樂)" (*Liji* 19.41; see also 19.27), as when you listen to a piece of good music, you cannot help but "to wave with your hands and dance with your feet" to the beat (*Liji* 19.45). Music is thus often contrasted with rites, as the latter is directed to one's outer behavior, while the former aims at one's inner feelings:

> when music (*yue* 樂) is used to cultivate one's heart/mind, the feelings of friendliness, uprightness, kindness, and sincerity will naturally arise; when such feelings arise, one will feel joy (*le* 樂); when one feels joy, one will be calm; when one is calm, one will be long-lasting [with one's virtuous inclination]; when one is long lasting, one will be in harmony with heaven; and when one is in harmony, one will be spiritual (*shen* 神). Heaven is trustworthy without speaking, and spirit is awesome without being angry. This is the achievement of cultivating one's heart/mind with music. (*Liji* 19.39)

In short, the function of music in moral education is that when one acts morally, one will not feel constrained by the external rules of propriety; instead, one acts spontaneously, effortlessly, and joyfully. This is indeed the realm that Confucius describes himself to be in after he turns 70: "act from one's heart/mind's desire without overstepping moral principles" (*Analects* 12.4).

In addition to the "Four Subjects," "Four Teachings," and "Six Classics," there is also a famous passage in the *Analects*: "aim at the way, rest on virtue, rely upon humanity, and effortlessly roam through arts" (*Analects* 7.6). It is commonly understood that "arts" here refers to the "Six Arts" (*liu yi* 六藝) taught in the official schools before and during Confucius's time: rites, music, archery, charioteering, calligraphy, and mathematics. However, I am not sure whether, in addition to rites and music that he taught through two of the six classics discussed above, Confucius also taught the other four, although he certainly mastered all six arts.[7] There are several reasons for this doubt. First, the "Six Classics" were sometimes also called "Six Arts," and so it is possible that in the above passage Confucius really talks about being extremely familiar with the six classics. This is possible, as only the six classics are on the same level of way, virtue, and humanity mentioned in the same passage. Second, even in the official schools, the six arts were regarded as lesser learning (*xiao xue* 小學) taught to beginners (children), to be followed by the six classics, which were regarded as great learning (*da xue* 大學), taught to advanced students. Third, in the *Analects*, there is no mention of the last two techniques, calligraphy and mathematics. While charioteering and archery are mentioned, they are not very highly valued. For example, in *Analects* 9.2, on hearing that he was indeed great and had broad learning but unfortunately had yet to earn a name in a specific field, Confucius said to his disciples, "what should I make myself proficient in? In archery or charioteering? Maybe I should choose charioteering."[8] This shows that for Confucius a person is great neither because he or she has any special skill in any specific field, nor because one has a broad learning, but because one is a person of humanity. These two techniques, according to Cai Shangsi, are necessary for military leadership.[9] However, when asked about military matters, Confucius says that "I have never learned anything about military" (*Analects* 15.1).[10]

From the above, it is clear that the primary goal of Confucius as an educator is not to transmit intellectual knowledge or technical skills to his students but to teach them how to be virtuous, authentic human beings.[11] This, of course, does not mean that Confucius is anti-intellectual or anti-technological. As a matter of fact, in addition to literary knowledge, Confucius also knows martial arts; he can run fast enough to catch a rabbit; and he can fish, hunt, raise cows and horses, do accounting, and run funerals. However, Confucius does not regard any of these as necessary for one to become a superior person. This is made clear in the following passage of the *Analects*:

> An official asked Zigong, "your master [Confucius] must be a sage; otherwise how could he be good at so many things?" Zigong replied, "It is true that Heaven has let him both be a sage and be good at many things." After hearing this, Confucius said, "This official knows me [about being good at many things]. When I was young I was of a humble station and acquired many basic skills. Do superior persons have to be good at many things? No, they do not." (*Analects* 9.6)

There has been disagreement about how to interpret the last two sentences (*Junzi duo hu zai* 君子多乎哉? *Bu duo ye* 不多也), with the last three characters here translated as "No. They do not" (see Cheng Shude 1990: 583). On the one extreme, it is believed that, for Confucius, a superior person ought not to have so many skills

("Ought superior persons to have so many skills? No, they ought not"); on the other extreme, it is believed that, for Confucius, a superior person is never worried about having too many skills ("Do superior persons complain about having too many skills? No, they do not") (see Chen Daqi 1969: 172). The one shows the incompatibility between having many skills and being a superior person, while the other regards it as necessary for a superior person to have many skills. However, I believe that from the context it is better to regard having many skills as neither necessary nor incompatible with being a sage.

This point can be better appreciated if we read it along with another passage: "Fan Chi asked to be taught how to grow crops. Confucius said, 'I am not as good as an experienced farmer on that.' Fan Chi asked to be taught how to garden. Confucius said, 'I am not as good as an experienced gardener.' After Fan Chi left, Confucius said, 'What an inferior person Fan Chi is! When those above love propriety, no common people dare be irreverent; when those above love rightness, no common people dare be disobedient; and when those above love trustworthiness, no common people dare be insincere" (*Analects* 3.4). Now, given what Confucius said in *Analects* 9.6 discussed above, it is perhaps not true that Confucius lacked farming and gardening skills. What is particularly relevant to our discussion is that it not only tells us what Confucius does not teach to his students, various skills, even if he possesses them, but also what he does teach his students: propriety, rightness, and trustworthiness.

There is a related short passage of merely four Chinese characters that is otherwise difficult to understand. Literally, it means that "a superior person is not a vessel (or instrument)" (*junzi bu qi* 君子不器) (*Analects* 2.12). Han Dynasty scholar Bao Xian's 包咸 (6–68) interpretation has been most influential: "vessels (*qi* 器) all have their respective uses, while a superior person is able to do everything" (in Cheng Shude: 96). Many commentators, including contemporary ones, accept this interpretation. For example, Qian Mu states that "vessels are like what we today call experts, while a superior person is one who is not limited to one capability or skill but is like what we today call an all-round person" (Qian 2005: 38). At my university, a new undergraduate major has been established for "general studies," in addition to existing majors in traditional specialized disciplines. According to the above interpretation, students majoring in "General Studies" would be superior persons or at least candidates for superior persons, while those majoring in traditional specialized disciplines could only end up being vessels. This is obviously not what Confucius means. In my view, its correct interpretation is hinted at by the neo-Confucian master Zhu Xi when he says that "vessels all have their respective and mutually exclusive uses, while a virtuous person is in one body with all and therefore can deal with everything" (see Cheng Shude 1990: 96). What is important here is that, instead of distinguishing between having one skill and having many skills, Zhu Xi makes a distinction between skills and virtues. A virtuous person can of course have one or more skills, but to learn to be a virtuous person is not to learn these skills. A virtuous person is not a vessel, because what the virtuous person has, virtue, can be exhibited whether the person is a teacher or a student, a ruler or minister, a parent or child, an artist or a technician, an astronomer or a doctor.[12]

4. Can virtue be taught and how?

We have seen that Confucius's education is moral education. In other words, the goal of his education is primarily not to make his students intellectually knowledgeable or technically skillful but to make them virtuous. Now, we can look at the puzzling statement of *Analects* 8.9 again: "common people can be made to do things but cannot be made to know things." It should be clear that the relevant knowledge is neither intellectual knowledge nor technical skills, but knowledge as virtue or virtue as knowledge, which is different from knowledge about virtue. When told that one should be virtuous (to love one's parents, for example), everyone understands what it means. This is knowledge about virtue, an intellectual understanding. However, when Confucius complains that "very few know virtue" (*Analects* 15.4), clearly he does not mean knowledge about virtue, but knowledge as virtue. Knowledge as virtue, for Confucius, has two features. The first is related to its source. Unlike knowledge about virtue, or intellectual knowledge in general, that only involves one's intellect, knowledge as virtue also involves one's heart; it needs a person's "own inner experience in knowing things" (*mo er shi zhi* 默而識之) (*Analects* 7.2). The second is related to its efficacy. It is not merely a cool understanding of virtue. It also inclines a person to act virtuously, to become a virtuous person. When Confucius says that people cannot be made to know things, he really means that people cannot be forced to be virtuous. You can force a person to do things, including virtuous things, but you cannot force a person to become virtuous.

Does this mean that Confucius's answer to Socrates's question, "can virtue be taught?" can only be negative? In appearance, it is the case, as Confucius stresses the importance of moral self-cultivation. For example, he states that "to practice humanity (*ren*) depends upon oneself, and not on others" (*Analects* 12.1), and he contrasts the ancient learners whom he admires and the present learners whom he looks down upon: "the ancient learners are for the sake of themselves [to cultivate their own virtues], while the present learners are for the sake of others [to show off what they have learned in front of others]" (*Analects* 14.24). He also asks us to "set higher standards for ourselves and make lighter demands upon others" (*Analects* 15.15) and to "attack our own badness instead of that of others" (*Analects* 12.21). He thus makes the contrast between superior persons and inferior persons: "the superior persons make demands upon themselves, while the inferior persons do so upon others" (*Analects* 15.21).[13]

However, this does not mean that, for Confucius, a virtuous person can only do virtuous things to others but cannot teach others to be virtuous. If so, his ethics would also suffer the so-called self-centeredness problem that some contemporary philosophers claim is inescapable for any versions of virtue ethics. However, as we have shown in Chapter Two, Confucius's ethics, also a version of virtue ethics, is certainly not self-centered in this sense. The whole purpose of a Confucian education is to make people virtuous. The most important virtue, the virtue that includes or at least leads all other virtues, for Confucius, is humanity (*ren* 仁). A person of humanity loves his or her children and is loyal to his or her parents, loves his or her younger siblings and is loyal to his or her older siblings, and loves his or her subordinates and is loyal to his or her superiors. However, for Confucius, to love or be loyal to someone is not merely to be concerned about their external well-being: "To love a person, don't you have to encourage the person to be good? To be loyal to someone, don't you have to remonstrate with the person?"

So, for Confucius, it is not the case that people cannot be made virtuous, but that they cannot be made virtuous in the same way as they can be made to do things; it is not the case that virtues cannot be taught, but that they cannot be taught in the same way as theoretical knowledge and technical skills are taught. In this respect, I think Chen Lai is right when he says that, "with respect to education in virtue, an educator's basic responsibility is to enlighten learners ... and inspire them to become superlative in character. The educator should arouse students to an admiration of exemplary persons and instill in them the desire to become this kind of consummate persons" (Chen Lai 2008: 322). Obviously, this cannot be done simply by issuing moral commands or even punitive laws, which can at most make people do virtuous things or refrain from doing vicious things but cannot make people virtuous.

The question is then how. We have already touched two ways Confucius uses to teach people to be virtuous. First, since the problem with nonvirtuous persons is that they do not have the motivation to be virtuous, and part of the reason they do not have the motivation to be virtuous is that they find it unpleasant to be virtuous, so, as Joel Kupperman points out, "Good education also requires some motivation on the part of the student in order to introduce a positive element of attraction to what otherwise might be experienced as dull and dispiriting. A sense of what the deep enjoyment is that is promised can be highly motivating. The fact that, as Confucian points out, these satisfactions are less vulnerable, adds to the motivational power" (Kupperman 2008: 408). Thus Confucius repeatedly emphasizes the joy brought to one by being virtuous, discussed above in relation to the function of music in moral education (see also Huang 2010a). Second, since what nonvirtuous persons lack is not an intellectual understanding of virtue but the sentiment or desire to be virtuous, it is important to stimulate such a sentiment or desire from them. As we have seen, for Confucius, poetry is important in moral education precisely because of this function, a function similar to the one played by the vivid, sad, and sentimental stories told by journalists, novelists, and reporters for Richard Rorty. For example, Rorty states that "the fate of women of Bosnia depends on whether television journalists manage to do for them what Harriet Beecher Stowe did for black slaves—whether these journalists can make us, the audience back in the safe countries, feel that these women are more like us, more like real human beings, than we had realized" (Rorty 1998: 180). In addition, in Chapter Five, Section 4, I shall discuss another way of moral education: remonstration. Although moral education is primarily done, as shown below, by parents to their children and rulers to their people, Confucius is also aware that sometimes parents and rulers may be morally deficient. In such cases, children and ministers become the moral teachers by remonstrating with their parents or rulers against any wrongdoing, when not done, and for correcting the wrong already done.

However, in the remainder of this section and the next section, I shall discuss in some detail the singular most important way to make people virtuous for Confucius, a way that also makes sense of some of his claims that apparently seem to say that a virtuous person should be only concerned about one's own being virtuous. This is teaching by being an exemplary person oneself. Thus, Confucius states, "when superior persons are diligent in being filial to their parents, common people will be stirred to humanity; and when superior persons do not forget their old friends, common people will not be cold to others" (*Analects* 8.2); and "when those above love propriety, common people do not dare be irreverent; when those above love rightness, common people do not dare be insubordinate; when those above love trustworthiness, common people do not dare be insincere. This way, common people from all places will come with their children strapped on their backs" (*Analects* 13.4).[14]

Confucius believes in the effectiveness of teaching with personal examples. Confucius says, "a virtuous person is not lonely; he or she must have people surrounding him" (*Analects* 4.25). In his view, a virtuous person's character and action are contagious, and so the person will necessarily have followers. Indeed it is in this context that we can understand the beginning passage of the *Analects*, consisting of three sentences, which are commonly understood as saying: "Is it not a pleasure to regularly review what one has learned? Is it not a joy to have friends come from afar? Is it not a superior person who does not feel any grudge when he or she is not known by others" (*Analects* 1.1). Such a banal understanding not only misses the important point Confucius wants to make but also obscures the important link among the three sentences. As what Confucius teaches and what his students learn is how to be a human, the term translated here as "review," *xi* 習, is to be understood as "practice." So the first sentence really means that it is a pleasure to put into practice what one has learned about how to become a virtuous human being (see Qian Mu 2001: 143–4). This is consistent with Confucius's emphasis on practice. As we have seen above, Confucius criticizes those who can recite all 300 poems in the *Book of Poetry* and yet cannot put what they have learned into practice (*Analects* 13.5). Moreover, this also reflects Confucius's view that virtuous action results in joy. For example, he says that "to know something is not as good as to love it [put it into practice], and to love it is not as good as to find joy in it" (*Analects* 6.20). Although it is not clearly stated what this "something is" (actually in the original Chinese text, the object of the three verbs, "know," "love," and "find joy in," is not mentioned), it is clear that Confucius means virtuous things. This is confirmed in another passage, in which Confucius reflects that "I can find joy even when I eat coarse rice, drink unboiled water, and sleep on my elbow as a pillow. I regard it as a passing cloud to have wealth and rank by being immoral" (*Analects* 7.16).

Now, in the second sentence, the term translated as friend, *peng* 朋, is to be understood as followers. Although in modern Chinese *peng* and *you* 友 synonymously, often used together as a compound word, mean friends, in the *Analects* the two terms are used differently. While *you* means friends, *peng* means comrades or followers. Thus I agree with the interpretation by Zhu Xi, who sees the second sentence as closely connected with the first. The first sentence says that one is happy in putting into practice what one has learned to become a virtuous person, and the second sentence says that one is happy because one's virtuous actions become contagious and so there are many followers. Moreover, Zhu claims that here one is not happy because the large number of followers shows that one is virtuous, "for since one already gets it, why should one be happy only after other people follow oneself? One should know that what one has got for oneself one also wants others to have. . . . When there are a lot of people following one (in becoming virtuous), how can one not be happy?" (Zhu 1986: 451). This interpretation is consistent with *Analects* 13.16, where Confucius says that a good ruler is one who "pleases those near and attracts those afar."

In this respect, we can see a significant difference between Confucius and Aristotle, at least according to one interpretation of the latter. There is an ambiguous passage in Aristotle's *Nichomachean Ethics*: the true self-lover, among other things, will "sacrifice actions to his friend, since it may be finer to be responsible for his friends' doing the action than to do it himself. In everything praiseworthy, then, the excellent person awards himself what is fine" (Aristotle: 1169a33–36). According to one interpretation, Aristotle is responding to the self-centeredness objection to virtue ethics, as he argues that a virtuous person, the true self-lover, shows concern for the virtue of others by sacrificing opportunities to perform virtuous actions to others. Christopher Toner explains what he thinks Aristotle says with a hypothetical scenario: two of us are friends and fellow members of a platoon engaged in a dangerous reconnaissance. One volunteer is needed to be the first to cross an open area. I am moved to volunteer, but I recall that you have unfairly acquired a reputation for cowardice and wanted to clear this reputation. Thus I remain silent so that you can be the first (see Toner 2006: 611). Richard Kraut provides a similar illustration: Suppose I think my friend is capable of supervising major civic projects, but that he has had too few opportunities to show his worth. I persuade public officials who oversee such projects to secure the opportunity for him (Kraut 1989: 126).

I have argued in a different place that, whether this is indeed what Aristotle means, a virtuous person cannot make a nonvirtuous person virtuous by sacrificing opportunities of performing virtuous actions to nonvirtuous persons (see Huang 2010c). I want to emphasize here that, from what we have discussed above, it is clear that this is not the way that Confucius recommends for virtuous people to make other people virtuous. For Confucius, while one should yield to others when faced with opportunities for external benefits, "when faced with the opportunities to practice virtues, one should not yield to the multitude" (*Analects* 15.36).[15] What Confucius has in mind is not what Richard Kraut, when discussing Aristotle's conception of friendship of virtues, calls "moral competition," in which all competitors may be winners. Rather, as Zhu Xi says in his comments on this passage, it is the occasion when one should be virtuous; there is no competition here, and so there should be no yielding (in Cheng Shude 1990: 1124). Moreover, unlike Aristotle's interest in relationship among virtuous friends, Confucius's main concern is the relationship between virtuous and nonvirtuous people. If virtuous persons yield in such situations, no one would do virtuous things, as the nonvirtuous persons, as nonvirtuous persons, would not do virtuous things either. In contrary, if the virtuous persons take the lead to be virtuous, then nonvirtuous persons may be morally moved and become virtuous.[16]

Of course, a virtuous person can become an exemplary person and thus can attract followers, that is, can have the effect of making others virtuous, only if the person and his or her virtuous actions are known by others. What happens if the person is not recognized by others and therefore does not have followers? This is what the third sentence is meant to say: a superior person does not feel any grudge against others. A common understanding of this sentence is that, for Confucius, the purpose of learning is self cultivation. So as long as one becomes virtuous, it really does not matter whether others know it or not (see Chen 1964: 5). Zhu Xi even uses the analogy of eating. One eats because one wants to get full, and there is no need to ask people whether they know that one is full (Zhu 1986: 453). There is some truth in that. However, for Confucius, a person is not only to be virtuous himself or herself but is also to help others to be virtuous. As a matter of fact, as we have shown in Chapter Two, a person cannot be regarded as virtuous unless one also wants to make others virtuous. So while one cannot complain about others for their failure to recognize one's virtues, one ought to complain about oneself for not being fully virtuous in the sense that one still lacks the transforming power upon nonvirtuous persons. In other words, the virtuous person will seek improvement within himself or herself instead of blaming others for not following oneself. This point is made repeatedly in the *Analects*. For example, Confucius says that "a superior person is troubled by one's own lack of ability rather than other people's failure to recognize him or her" (*Analects* 15.19; see also 14.30), and that "one should be concerned not about not having an official position but about one's lack for qualification for the position; and one should be concerned not about other people's failure to appreciate you but about one's lack of things worthy of appreciation" (*Analects* 4.14). All these are consistent with a central point I have made in Chapter Two: a virtuous person will see the very existence of a single nonvirtuous person as an indication that he or she has not fully fulfilled his or her responsibility.

5. The role of government in moral education

Analects 2.3 is the most famous saying of Confucius on the function of government recorded in the *Analects*: "If you guide people with coercive measures and keep them in line with punishment, then they will stay out of trouble but will have no sense of shame. If you guide them with virtue and keep them in line with ritual propriety, then they will have a sense of shame and rectify themselves" (*Analects* 2.3). It must be pointed out that Confucius's problem with governing by coercive measures and punishment is not that they are not effective. They are quite effective in terms of preventing people from doing immoral things. His concern is rather that the common people thus governed, while law-abiding, would become shameless. Governing with ritual propriety and virtue can have the same effect of preventing people from wrongdoings, but Confucius advocates it because people governed this way will have a sense of shame. In other words, for Confucius, the primary function of government is the moral education of its people. It is here that we see a stark contrast between Confucius and contemporary political liberals in terms of the function of government.

Liberalism in contemporary political philosophy is unique, at least partly because it emphasizes a strict division between the political and the personal. This division has two sides. The first is that "the personal is not political": The function of government is limited to people's lives in the public sphere, while their lives in the private sphere, particularly within family, are "protected" from governmental interventions. The problem with this claim has been fully detected by many feminist thinkers. Feminists are right in insisting that the personal is political, which, of course, does not mean that the government can be omnipresently intrusive. However, the liberal division between the political and the personal has a second implication, which is not grasped by such feminists under the slogan "the personal is political," and therefore its related problem is not only unidentified by them but is (or will be) further perpetrated by the very procedures they propose to alleviate the injustice within the personal sphere. In this liberal tradition, not only is the personal not political, but the political is also not personal: the function of government is limited to establishing social institutions regulated by just laws and public policies but has nothing to do with the types of persons living within these institutions. In other words, its job is to improve the social institutions so that they are fair to every individual living within the institutions but not to cultivate the virtues of these individuals and, of course, not to make them vicious. This liberal idea is problematic.

In appearance, since the liberal tradition insists that the political is not personal, if it is not conducive to cultivating virtues of individuals, we may think that at least it does not induce vices. It leaves persons as they are. It simply makes rules fair to all who play the games governed by these rules. This, however, is not true. In his criticism of liberalism in general and Rawls's theory of justice in particular, G. A. Cohen claims that "social structures extensively shape the structure of motivation," because human nature is quite "plastic with respect to motivation" (Cohen: 119). In his view, the liberal society not only does nothing to reshape human nature to make it good, it actually encourages people to be selfish. He particularly has in mind Rawls's difference principle, part of his second principle of justice, which provides a justification of social and economic inequality: the most talented, if not given more, will not make full use of their talents, and, as a result, everyone else will become worse off. So, Rawls argues, it is fair to let the most talented have the right amount of the extra that is enough and no more than enough to motivate them to make full use of their talents so that everyone else in the society can benefit from it. In Cohen's view, this principle not only encourages the selfishness of the most talented: we (the most talented) will not make the greatest contribution we can to society if we are not allowed to receive a greater share of goods than the rest; it also encourages the selfishness of the least advantaged: we will not allow the most talented to have a greater share if we cannot benefit more from their exercising their talents (see Cohen: chapter 8).

All this has shown to us is that liberals are simply wrong to think that the political is not personal. The political is personal: a particular kind of government will not only determine the kind of society but also determine, to a great extent, the kind of people who live in the society. It is in this context that we can appreciate the significance of Confucius's political philosophy, as it makes it explicit that the function of government is the moral education of its people. Moreover, for Confucius, government performs this function primarily through the exemplary behaviors of the rulers rather than rules the rulers make, and it is in this sense that Confucius's view is also significantly different from Aristotle's view, which is sometimes used as an alternative to liberal political theories today, as Aristotle thinks that government does have the function of moral education of citizens. However, Aristotle's theory has two unique features. The first is his claim that moral education is the job of legislators instead of, rather than in addition to, private citizens (such as parents and friends), even though legislators normally do not have as intimate knowledge of citizens as parents have of their children or friends have of their friends and are not necessarily more virtuous than a parent or friend. This is related to the second feature of Aristotle's theory: the legislators perform their role of moral education not through their exemplary behaviors for people to emulate but through the laws they make. In Aristotle's view, "it is difficult to get from youth up a right training for virtue if one has not been brought up under right laws; for to live temperately and hardily is not pleasant to most people, especially when they are young. For this reason their nurture and occupations should be fixed by law" (Aristotle: 1180a19–20); and he further points out that most people "do not by nature obey the sense of shame, but only fear, and do not abstain from bad acts because of their baseness but through fear of punishment" (Aristotle: 1179b11–13). So Aristotle and contemporary liberals agree that the primary function of government is to make punitive laws. The difference is that, while liberals claim that the laws are neutral with regard to people's characters: they will not make people either virtuous or vicious, Aristotle argues that punitive laws can and should make people virtuous.

In both respects Confucius disagrees with Aristotle. Confucius does distinguish between private virtuous persons and political leaders in terms of their roles in moral education. Political rulers can play their role in moral education precisely because an individual virtuous person can play such a role. So just like private persons can make others virtuous only through their own exemplary virtuous actions, political rulers can make common people virtuous

also only through their own exemplary virtuous actions. The reason that Confucius emphasizes the importance of political rulers in
moral education is primarily not because they can do so through
any political and legal measures, which a private virtuous person
cannot do, but simply because their actions will be emulated by
all people they govern, while a private person's exemplary virtuous
actions can only affect those who are near.

It is for this reason that, in his advice to political rulers, Confucius
repeatedly emphasizes the importance of being virtuous. For example, he says that "if the ruler makes oneself correct, what difficulty
will the ruler have to govern people? If the ruler cannot make oneself
correct, how can the ruler make others correct?" (*Analects* 13.13).
In this passage, the term for "govern" is *zheng* 政, which is a cog-
nate of the word for "correct," *zheng* 正. Thus, in another passage,
when Ji Kangzi ask about government, Confucius says that "to
govern (*zheng* 政) is to be correct (*zheng* 正). If you [a ruler] are
correct, who dare be not correct" (*Analects* 12.17); Ji Kangzi was
worried about burglary, and Confucius advised him: "If you yourself
were not one with desire [to steal things from your people], no one
would steal even if you reward them for stealing" (*Analects* 12.18);
Ji Kangzi further asked whether it would be OK to kill people who
do not follow *Dao*, and Confucius replies: "why do you need to kill
in governing? If you want to be good, then your people will be good.
The nature of the superior person is like wind, while the nature of
inferior person is like grass. When the wind blows, the grass will
bend" (*Analects* 12.19). For Confucius, if a ruler "is correct, then no
commands are issued and yet people all follow, while if the ruler is
not correct, then even if commands are issued, people will not obey"
(*Analects* 13.6); "a ruler who governs by being virtuous himself can
be compared to the Polar Star which commands homage of the multitude without leaving its place" (*Analects* 2.1).[17]

Of course, while Confucius was an idealist, he was not a utopian.
He realized that it takes time before punitive laws can be entirely
abandoned. He speaks highly of the saying "Let good people govern a state for one hundred years, and there will be no need for cruelty and death penalty" (*Analects* 13.11). This shows that for a long
period, even when a state is governed by good people, there is still
need for punitive laws. However, Confucius's ideal is that such laws
are made but never used (*Kongzi Jiayu* 1; 1). Thus he states, "The
purpose that sages establish deterring measures is that they will not

be violated. The supreme government is one that has the five types of punishment and yet never uses them. . . . When there are such measures, people know where to stop, and when they know where to stop, they will not violate them. Thus, although there are punishments for trickery, wickedness, burglary, robbery, and defying laws, there are no people being punished for these" (*Kongzi Jiayu* 30; 1). Clearly for Confucius, punitive laws are mainly to deter bad people from doing bad things and not as a trap. So it is very important at the same time when bad people are deterred by these punitive laws from doing bad things, they should also be taught to be virtuous. Perhaps reflecting upon his experience as the minister of justice, Confucius himself says that "in terms of deciding on legal cases, I'm just about the same as other people. What is important is to eliminate the cause of such legal cases" (*Analects* 12.13).

When such legal cases indeed arise, Confucius also thinks it important to seek alternatives to legal decisions if possible. When Confucius was minister of justice in the state of Lu, there was a legal case between father and son, with the former suing the latter for not being filial. Confucius put them in the same room for 3 months without judging the case. The father eventually asked to withdraw the case, and Confucius let them go. When asked why he let the son free instead of punishing him, as Confucius himself taught the importance of filial piety to rule a state, Confucius stated, "it is not right for those above to kill those below instead of teaching them. It amounts to punishing the innocent to decide the case without first teaching them filial piety. When your soldiers retreat in defeat, you cannot stop it with the threat of killing them; and when criminal cases come in multitude, you cannot eliminate them by severe punishment. Why? Because the problem is not with people but with the ruler who fails to teach" (*Kongzi Jiayu* 2; 7; see also *Xunzi* 28.3).

Confucius thus further contrasts his ideal ancient society, where "there were deterring power and penal punishments but they were never used," with the contemporary society in which he lived, where "moral education is distorted, and penal laws are complicated, but common people are confused and trapped into places, receiving penal punishments. Therefore the more complicated the penal laws are, the more thieves and robbers emerge" (*Kongzi Jiayu* 2; 15). Of course, Confucius does not want to abandon the penal punishment altogether, but punishment must be preceded as well as followed by moral education. In his view, "teaching must come before penal punishment. One should first cultivate people's moral virtues; if this does not work, one should promote worthy persons as exemplar for people to follow; if this still does not work, one should demote unworthy persons; if this still does not work, then one should use power to deter them. In three years, people will be rectified. If there are still some people not transformed after all these, then one can apply the penal punishment, as they will all know the crime they committed" (*Kongzi Jiayu* 2; 7–8).

However, even when penal punishment as a last resort becomes necessary, there are two important things that a political leader must keep in mind. First, the punishment should not primarily be retributive, returning to the criminal the harm the criminal inflicted upon others, but a measure to transform the criminal. Confucius thus makes this following contrast between the ancient society and his own society, with the former being preferred: "ancient law enforcement aimed to minimize the law-breaking cases, which is the root, while present law enforcement aims to not let any law-breakers free, which is branch"; and "present judges seek the way to punish people, while judges in the ancient time sought the way to let people live" (*Kongzi Jiyu* 408). Second, and more importantly, judges of course ought to do what they can to ensure that they make the right legal decisions. However, even when they rule that a person indeed committed the crime charged, Confucius advised that they "should not congratulate themselves [for getting the truth] but should instead have a feeling of sadness and compassion (*an jin wu xi* 哀矜勿喜)" (*Analects* 19.19).[18] In another place, Confucius says something similar: "when making a legal decision, even though one gets clear about the fact that a person commits the crime, one must have the feeling of sadness and compassion about the person. The life of a person receiving capital punishment cannot be restored, and the part of a person's body being cut off as a punishment cannot be reconnected. That is the reason that the *Book of Documents* talks about 'making legal decision with the feeling of sadness and compassion'" (*Kongzi Jiyu* 368). The reason that one ought to have such a feeling of sadness and compassion is that one ought to realize that one fails to successfully educate the person to render punishment unnecessary but instead has to appeal to it as the last resort. This is what Rosalind Hursthouse calls moral remainder or residue: some kind of guilt, remorse, or regret a virtuous person feels when he or she has done a thing that he or she has to do and that is the best thing to do but is something he or she would rather not do in an ideal world (Hursthouse 1999: 75–6). This is similar to what Laozi says about war. Laozi is generally anti-war. However, when a good ruler finds war unavoidable and fights a victorious war, he does not regard it as praiseworthy but observes the occasion with funeral ceremonies, not only for the people who died for him but also for people from the opposing side who died (*Laozi* 31).

Such a feeling of sadness, guilt, regret, or remorse itself is also praiseworthy, since a person's virtue is not only manifested in one's action but also in one's emotion. At the same time, such a moral residue or remainder may also exert its moral transforming power. In *Kongzi Jiayu*, there is a story that illustrates this point well. A palace coup in the state of Wei caused chaos. Ji Gao, a state official in charge of execution of punishment, was fleeing the capital to find a safe place, when he recognized that the gatekeeper was one he had punished. The gatekeeper told Ji Gao to escape over a broken wall; Ji Gao refused, saying that a gentleman would not jump over a wall. The gatekeeper then suggested a hole under the wall; again, Ji Gao refused, saying that a gentleman would not do so. Finally he was told that there was a room to hide himself in. Ji Gao got into this room and was safe in the chaos. When the coup was over and Ji Gao came out, he asked the gatekeeper: "I punished you before, and so it was a good time for you to take revenge. But you didn't and instead helped me find a safe place. Why?" The man replied that "the punishment you gave me was what I deserve; and I saw you felt worried and sad when you made the decision to punish me." Having heard this story, Confucius said, "How wonderful. There is the only way to be officials. Benevolence and altruism within yourself will result in virtues in others, and cruel and harsh actions will result in misgivings in others" (*Kongzi Jiayu* 8; 39).

6. Conclusion

Confucius has often been regarded as the first private teacher in Chinese history. However, as our examination above has shown, he was not a teacher in the conventional sense, as the content of his teaching is neither intellectual knowledge nor technical skills but the way to become a virtuous person. While Confucius fully realizes that a person can become virtuous ultimately only by himself or herself, he does think that there are a number of things that a virtuous person can do to help others become virtuous, the most important of which is to be a virtuous exemplar. Such a function can of course be performed by any individual virtuous person, but Confucius pays more attention to political leaders, as their influence is much wider and deeper. For this reason, in Confucius's political philosophy, the primary function of government is the moral education of its people, which stands in stark contrast to contemporary political liberalism; moreover, the government performs this function of moral education primarily not through laws and other political measures but through the rulers' being moral exemplars themselves, which is in sharp contrast with Aristotle's vision. In Confucius's view, while laws and punishment cannot be entirely thrown out yet, they should be used merely as temporary and supplementary measures. Even when such measures become inevitable, a virtuous political leader will exhibit a natural feeling of sadness, no less about the leader's own inability to transform the vicious person through other measures than about the regrettable status of the vicious person.

CHAPTER FIVE

Filial piety: Why an upright son does not disclose his father stealing a sheep

1. Introduction

In Chapter One, in our discussion of Confucius's visit to the state of Chu, we recorded a conversation between the governor of She and Confucius. The governor told Confucius, clearly with some pride, "in our village there is an upright person, Zhigong. He bears witness against his father stealing a sheep." Confucius responded, "in my village, an upright person is different: father does not disclose son's wrongdoing, and son does not disclose father's wrongdoing, and the uprightness is in it" (*Analects* 13.18). This longstanding controversial conversation is the focus of a heated debate on Confucian ethics in mainland China during the last decade or so.[1] Conceivably, critics of Confucian ethics see Confucius unjustifiably trumping social justice with family feeling, while defenders emphasize the value of genuine family love, particularly that of filial piety, not only in and of itself but also for social justice, as the former is regarded as the root of the latter. In this chapter, I shall make a new attempt to make sense of this controversial conversation. However, since this is closely related to Confucius's idea of filial piety, I shall examine the three unique senses of Confucius's conception of filial piety (Sections 2–4) before I move on to the conversation itself (Section 5). The chapter will conclude with a brief summary.

2. Filial piety I: reverence and love

The Chinese character for filial piety, *xiao* 孝, consists of a top part of the character for the elderly, *lao* 老, and the character for child, *zi* 子, on the bottom. The earliest form of the character looks like an elderly person (parent) helped by a cane (the child) to walk. According to *Shuowen Jiezi* 說文解字, the most authoritative dictionary of ancient Chinese characters, filial piety means being good at serving one's parents, particularly in terms of their physical needs. For this reason, among the five types of son commonly regarded as not filial that Mencius mentions, the first three are all related to their failure to take care of their parents' physical needs: "the first are those who are lazy to do anything and thus neglect their parents' livelihood; the second are those who are indulgent in gambling, gaming, and drinking and thus neglect their parents' livelihood; the third are those who are stingy with their money and property and partial toward their wives and thus neglect their parents' livelihood; the fourth are those who are indulgent in sensual pleasure and therefore bring shames to their parents; and the fifth are those who are quarrelsome and truculent and then endanger their parents" (*Mencius* 4b30).[2] Confucius certainly agrees that it is important for a filial child to take good care of the physical needs of his or her parents, as otherwise one would be worse than an animal. However, Confucius emphasizes that such care be accompanied by appropriate feelings or emotions.[3]

In *Analects* 2.7, Ziyou, one of Confucius's students, asks about filial piety, and Confucius replies, "Nowadays to be filial merely means to take care of our parents' physical needs. However, even dogs and horses can provide [or receive] such care. If there is a lack of reverence, where does the difference lie?" In this passage, the middle sentence is subject to three different interpretations, and my translation is intentionally made ambiguous so that, to varying degrees, it can convey any of the three meanings. According to the interpretation taken by Huang Kan 皇侃 (488–545), even dogs and horses can provide care to our parents, as dogs can guard the house and horses can take burdens off them. Of course, they don't have reverence for one's parents. So if we merely take care of our parents without reverence, then there is no difference between our care for our parents and the animals' care for our parents (in Cheng Shude:

86). The problem with this interpretation is that, strictly speaking, we cannot say dogs and horses are taking care of our parents; rather it is our parents who are making use of them.

The second interpretation was offered by Zhu Xi 朱熹 (1130–1200), according to which it means that we also take care of dogs and horses; thus, if we take care of our parents without reverence, there is no difference between our taking care of parents and our taking care of dogs and horses (in Cheng Shude: 86). The problem with this interpretation, as pointed out by the Qing Dynasty scholar Li Guangdi 李光地 (1642–1718), is that Confucius would not make such an inappropriate analogy between dogs and horses on the one hand and our parents on the other, both taken care of by us without reverence. In comparison it is relatively not problematic to make the analogy, as in the first interpretation, between dogs and horses on the one hand and some human beings, who both take care of the latter's parents without reverence. Those human beings who take care of their parents without reverence, as inferior persons (*xiaoren* 小人), may indeed be not much different from dogs or horses. For example, Confucius makes the following contrast between superior persons and inferior persons: "even inferior persons can also take care of their parents' physical needs. If superior persons lack reverence toward their parents, what is the distinction?" (*Liji* 30.12). So those who serve their parents without reverence are inferior people; and since inferior people are often regarded as not much different from animals, we can conclude that inferior persons' care of their parents is not much different from animals' care of their old.

So Li Guangdi, in his *Notes on the* Analects (*Lunyu Zhaji* 論語劄記) proposes a third interpretation, according to which it means that dogs and horses can also take care of their (dogs' and horses') parents; if we human beings take care of our parents without reverence, there is no difference between our taking care of our parents and dogs and horses taking care of their respective old. Cheng Shude 程樹德 (1877–1944) speaks very highly of this interpretation, saying that while Li's *Notes on the Analects* as a whole is superficial and hardly useful, this particular interpretation is not only novel but also superior to alternative interpretations (Cheng Shude: 86). However Yang Bojun 楊伯峻 (1909–92) claims that this interpretation is also problematic: as a matter of fact, dogs and horses do not take care of their respective parents, and Confucius would not make such a common sense mistake (Yang Bojun 1980: 15). Li Guangdi, however, seems to have anticipated this objection, and so he makes it clear that Confucius uses "dogs and horses" to refer to animals in general, and if so, what Confucius says is not false. Not only are there animals that take care of their young, as pointed out by Xunzi, "a nursing sow does not anger a tiger, and a nursing dog does not wander far away, as they do not forget their young to be taken care of" (*Xunzi* 4.3); there are also animals that take care of their old, as there are stories about a crow's feeding its old to return the care received when young and a lamb's kneeling down when receiving the milk from its old to express its gratitude, as collected in the popular classical essay, "*A Worthy Essay to Expand Our Knowledge*" (*Zeng Guan Xian Wen* 增廣賢文).

While all three interpretations agree that it is important that we ought to have the feeling of reverence toward one's parents when we take care of them, it seems to me that the third interpretation not only makes the best sense but also has an added significance. Contemporary evolutionary biology and evolutionary psychology have shown that animals and human beings form a continuum in terms of their altruistic concerns. For example, prairie dogs send out alarm calls to warn the group of perceived dangers, female lions suckle cubs of other lionesses, primates engage in grooming behavior to rid members of their troop of parasites, and soldier aphids forego their own reproduction for the sake of the cline mates (see Bertram 1976; Ridley and Dawkins 1981: 42–43; and Silk, Samuels, and Rodman 1981). Based on such recognition, Mary Midgley goes so far to claim that "we are not just like animals; we are animals" (Midgley 1995: xiii). It is interesting that Confucius perceived this continuity 2,500 years ago. Further, and more important, he also recognized and emphasized the difference: while both humans and (at least some) animals can take care of their respective old, what makes humans different from animals is that they have reverence toward their parents when they are taking care of them.

However, it is possible to be reverent to our parents without feeling love for them, and for Confucius, to be reverent without the feeling of love is not genuine filial piety. This point is made clear when he says, with rulers in mind, that "if they love their parents, they would not hate the parents of others; and if they are reverent toward their parents, they would not be arrogant to the parents of others" (*Xiaojing* 3). In this sense, Cai Yuanpei 蔡元培 (1868–1940) is correct when he says that "love and reverence are the longitude and latitude respectively of filial piety. . . . Without love, reverence becomes strange, and without reverence, love becomes perverse" (Cai 1999: 38–9; Quoted in Guo 2011: 2). This is the point Confucius makes in the passage immediately following in the *Analects*, in which he replies to another of his students about filial piety: "what is difficult is facial expression. The young's taking on the burden when there are things to be done and letting the old enjoy food and wine when they are available can hardly be regarded as filial piety" (*Analects* 2.8). What is clear in this passage is that facial expression is more important than doing things for and providing things to one's parents. What is not clear is what Confucius means by "facial expressions." Traditionally there are two groups of interpretation, one viewing it as the facial expressions of children serving their parents, and the other regarding it as the facial expressions of parents being served. The former is the so-called "taking care of our parents with our appropriate facial expression (*yang se* 養色)," while the latter is the so-called "taking care of our parents by observing their intention (*yang zhi* 養志)," and both are regarded as superior to merely taking physical care of one's parents (*yang ti* 養體).[4]

On the one hand, according to Zhu Xi, who follows the interpretation by Han Dynasty scholar Zheng Xuan 鄭玄 (127–200), Confucius is concerned about the facial expression we ought to have in serving our parents. In his view, facial expressions naturally reflect what we truly feel in our inner heart. Thus, commenting on this passage, he points out that "a filial person who has deep love for his or her parents must be gentle, a gentle person must be amiable, and an amiable person must have pleasant facial expression. Therefore, in serving our parents, it is difficult to maintain a pleasant facial expression [without deep love]. To merely take physical care of our parents is not enough to be regarded as filial" (in Cheng Shude: 90). Liu Yuan 劉沅 (1767–1855) makes a similar point from a different perspective: "we ought to have deep love for our parents with a gentle heart; even though we may be concerned with other things, we become pleasant and kind upon seeing our parents, with all worries forgotten" (in Cheng Shude: 89). According to Qian Dian 錢坫 (1744–1806), a filial person with deep love for his or her parents will naturally have a pleasant facial expression upon knowing his or her parents are healthy and a facial expression of concern upon knowing that his or her parents are not well (in Cheng Shude: 89). While with different emphases, these commentators all connect what we feel from our inner heart to what we express in our face. Without deep love for our parents inside, even if we are taking care of our parents, we cannot have the appropriate natural facial expressions outside.

This interpretation is consistent with what Confucius says on a couple of other occasions, although not recorded in the *Analects*. On one occasion, in responding to a question from his student Zilu, "there is a person who, in serving his parents, gets up early and goes to sleep late, working so hard in growing crops that his hands and feet are full of thick callus. Yet, he is still not regarded as filial. Why?" Confucius replies: "I think it is perhaps because his conduct is not reverent, his language is not modest, and his facial expression is not pleasing" (*Kongzi Jiayu* 22; 150). Here the first cause mentioned is related to reverence discussed above, while the second two, particularly the last one, are related to the facial expression that this current *Analects* passage means. On another occasion, Confucius says that "in serving their parents, filial children ought to be reverent in daily life, express their joy in providing their parents with physical care, show their concerns when their parents are sick, feel sad when their parents die, and be serious in worshipping them" (*Xiaojing* 10). While the first sentence is about being reverent, the rest are all about the expressions filial children ought to have in serving their parents on various occasions.

On the other hand, according to the two Han Dynasty classicists Bao Xian 包咸 (7 BCE–65) and Ma Rong 馬融 (79–166), what Confucius has in mind is the facial expressions of the parents. Thus, for Bao Xian, what Confucius says is that it is easy to do work for one's parents and provide food and drink to them, but "it is difficult to serve them according to their facial expressions" (in Cheng Shude: 90). Ma Rong even states that "to simply do work for and provide food and drink to one's parents is not real expression of filial piety; to be filial, one ought to serve them according to their facial expressions" (in Cheng Shude: 90). This interpretation emphasizes that to be filial, we ought to know the needs of our parents simply from their facial expressions even without their telling us. Whether or not this is indeed what Confucius means, it is certainly an important aspect of filial piety. As we know, among

Confucius's students, Zengzi is famous for his virtue of filial piety. When asked whether he can be regarded as filial, however, Zengzi responds, clearly with modesty: "How can you say that? How can you say that? Superior people regard it as filial to know what one's parents think before they say it and to guide them with the Way. I simply take care of the physical needs of my parents. How can it be regarded as filial?" (*Da Dai Liji* 52). Of the two items that Zengzi mentions here as true filial piety, while "to guide parents with the Way" is related to remonstration to be discussed in Section 4, "to know what one's parents think before they say it" is closely related to the *Analects* passage we discuss here, as this can only be done by observing their facial expressions. As soon as one knows what one's parents think, Zengzi says that "a filial child, in serving his or her parents, ought to make them feel happy and not go against their desires" (*Liji* 12.32). To be able to do so, Zengzi further points out that a filial child "ought not to have his or her own worry or joy"; instead he or she "ought to worry about what his or her parents worry about and feel joy about what his or her parents feel joy about" (*Da Dai Liji* 53) and "to love those one's parents love and respect those one's parents respect" (*Liji* 12.32).

So for Confucius, a filial person of course ought to take care of his or her parents; it is itself not something easy to accomplish. However, what makes human beings' care of their parents different from (some) animals' care of their old is that human beings' care of their parents is accompanied and supplemented by appropriate emotions. This is consistent with our conception of a virtuous person. A virtuous person is not merely a person who does virtuous things. After all, a nonvirtuous person may also do such things. What makes a virtuous person different from a nonvirtuous person is that the virtuous person's action is accompanied and/or supplemented by appropriate emotions. For example, as Rosalind Hursthouse, a contemporary (neo)Aristotelian virtue ethicist, points out, "we think of honest people as people who tend to avoid the dishonest deeds and do the honest ones in a certain manner—readily, eagerly, unhesitatingly, scrupulously, as appropriate. . . . And this spills over into the emotions we expect from them. We expect them to be distressed when those near and dear to them are dishonest, to be unresentful of honest criticism, to be surprised, shocked, and angered (as appropriate) by flagrant acts of dishonesty, not to be amused by certain tales of chicanery, to despise rather than to envy those who succeed by dishonest means, to be unsurprised or pleased, or delighted (as appropriate) when honesty triumphs" (Hursthouse 1999: 12).

3. Filial piety II: self-cultivation

Filial piety is commonly understood as what we ought to do for and feel about our parents. However, in an important sense it is also inseparable from our self-cultivation. Confucius makes this point in his response to Meng Wubo's 孟武伯 question about filial piety as recorded in *Analects* 2.6.

This passage has been subject to two very different interpretations. It could either mean that the only worry parents have about their children is their children's being ill or that the only worry the children have about their parents is their parents' being ill. In appearance, since this is Confucius's reply to a question about filial piety, it should be children's worry about their parents being sick, not parents' worry about their children's being sick. This is indeed one of the main reasons that Chen Daqi 陳大奇 (1886–1983) adopts this interpretation, claiming that while the former shows children's filial piety toward parents, the latter only indicates parents' kindness toward children (Chen 1969: 19). However, there are some problems with this interpretation. First, in the original Chinese sentence with the seven Chinese characters, "*fumu* 父母 (parents) *wei* 唯 (only) *qi* 其 (their) *ji* 疾 (disease) *zhi* 之 (an assisting word to indicate that the object of the verb, "disease," is before the verb, "worry") *you* 憂 (worry)," it is more natural to understand the two characters for "parents" at the very beginning as the subject rather than the object of the verb "worry." Second, if parents are the object of the verb, then it repeats the pronoun *qi*. Moreover, understood this way, the parents' illness becomes the only worry that children ought to have about their parents, but Confucius mentioned additional things for children to worry about.

Thus, despite the initial appearance, this understanding can also be seen as a proper answer to Meng Wubo's question about children's filial piety toward parents and not parents' kindness toward children. While it refers to parents' worry over their children's health, it really means that children should not let their parents have any worry about them except their having a disease. All parents wish their children well in all aspects, and so filial children, who love their parents, should not disappoint them or cause them to have any worry, except having a disease, which is not within their control. Moreover, as we know, unlike Socrates, who is interested in searching for a universal definition in any inquiry, Confucius always gives a reply that is appropriate to the person who asks the questions. Thus, in the *Analects*, many people ask him about filial piety, and in each case he gives a different answer. So presumably, Confucius's answer in this passage must also be particularly relevant to Meng Wubo, who asks the question. What kind of person is Meng Wubo? He was the son of Meng Yizi 孟懿子, sent by his father to study with Confucius, and one of the three hereditary ministers who controlled the state of Lu. According to Cheng Shude, "growing up within such a wealthy and powerful family, Meng Wubo has all sorts of moral faults such as arrogance, profligacy, licentiousness, laziness," etc. that bring shame to his parents (Cheng Shude: 84). To get rid of such moral faults, unlike ensuring that one is physically healthy, is within everyone's control, and so one should not allow them to become causes of his or her parents' worry.

Perhaps for this reason, the interpretation adopted here is also the one taken by the majority of classical and contemporary commentators of the *Analects*. For example, Han Dynasty classicist Ma Rong 馬融 (79–166) says that this sentence means that "a filial son is not to be preposterous and to commit wrongdoing. Only his disease may cause his parents to worry" (see Cheng Shude: 84). The Southern Dynasty classicist Huang Kan 皇侃 (488–545) agrees that this passage "means that children want to be always serious and cautious, not to do anything illegal, when they are away from their parents, in order not to cause their parents to have any worry"; and he further explains that "if they have diseases [which also cause their parents to worry], this is the only thing that children as human beings cannot do anything about" (see Cheng Shude: 84). However, it is the Qing Dynasty scholar Li Zhongfu 李中孚 (1627–1705) who makes the most detailed comments on this *Analects* passage in this respect:

> Parents worry about their children having disease in their physical bodies, to say nothing about their heart-mind. So if

they cannot take good care of their hearts-minds and allow them to have disease, then their guilt of the lack of filiality cannot be exonerated. . . . Parents are not only worried about their children's being hungry, cold, and tired but also about their other diseases, such as their virtues not cultivated, their career not elevated, their estrangement from right path and being close to the wickedness, their making friends with bad people, their negligence in examination of themselves, and their having improper words and deeds. Only if they know that these are also diseases and keep them away from themselves can they relieve their parents from worries and live up to the name of filial children. (In Cheng Shude: 85)

A more contemporary scholar, Cai Yuanpei, makes a similar point when he states, "Parents not only wish their children healthy but also wish them honored. If children are mediocre and incompetent, cannot fulfill their duties to their country and society, and even acquire a habit of doing immoral things to make their parent feel ashamed, then the parents will have a strong feeling of guilt and anger. How can children make their parents happy?" (Cai 1999: 41, Quoted in Guo 2011: 3).

So according to *Analects* 2.6, since parents are happy if their children are doing well but will worry when they do not do well, a filial son ought to avoid doing anything that his parents will be ashamed of and do only things that his parents can feel proud of. To interpret *Analects* 2.6 this way, we don't mean that to worry about parents' having a disease or to take care of one's own physical body is not the content of filial piety. They both certainly are. What we need to emphasize is that, for Confucius, to be a virtuous person oneself is also an important aspect of filial piety, because parents all wish their children well in all aspects.[5] It is in this sense that we can understand why Mencius regards the sage king Shun as an exemplar of filial piety: "the greatest thing a filial son can do is to bring honor to his parents, and the greatest thing a filial son can do to honor his parents is to serve them by being the ruler of the empire. To be the father of the son of heaven is the greatest honor a father can receive, and to serve one's parents by being the ruler of the empire is the greatest way a son can serve his parents" (*Mencius* 5a4).

There are two sources outside *the Analects* that record Confucius's sayings that support our interpretation. One is in the *The Senior Dai's Book of Rites*: "It is said in the *Book of Poetry* that 'there are seven sons, none of whom can make their mother free of worry.' This is sons' reflection upon their own guilt. It is also said in the *Book of Poetry* that 'working diligently by getting up early and going to sleep late can avoid making their parents feel ashamed.' This is about the sons' not giving up. Not to make one's parents feel ashamed of oneself is the superior person's way of filial piety" (*Da Dai Liji* 51). It is important to note here that neither what sons fail to do nor what they diligently do are things directed to their parents; rather they are directed to the filial children themselves. However, precisely because they are so, they are also indirectly directed to their parents. This is because, as we mentioned, parents are concerned with their children's well-being, physical, mental, and moral. Thus, on the one hand, when children fail to take care of themselves in any of these aspects, they disappoint their parents and bring shame to them. This shows a lack of filial piety; on the other hand, when children take good care of themselves in these aspects, they make their parents happy and bring honor to them. This shows great filial piety.

The other source is in the *Book of Filial Piety*, which regards it as the highest stage of filial piety. Confucius tells Zengzi: "One dare not harm one's body as this is given by one's parents. This is the beginning of filial piety. One establishes oneself and practices the Way so that one maintains a good reputation in history to illuminate one's parents. This is the end of filial piety" (*Xiaojing* 1). As we just noted, when Confucius speaks to his students, he normally does not make general statements but always has the particularities of his students in mind. Zengzi is known for his exemplary filial piety, and one way in which he is filial is to take good care of his own physical body. This is because one's body for him "is continuation of parents' bodies. Moving the parents' body around, how can one be without reverence?" (*Da Dai Liji* 52). To this end, Zengzi goes so far as to say that "a filial person does not climb up to the high place, go to the dangerous place, or stand at the verge of steep cliff" (*Da Dai Liji* 50); and a filial son, "walking, takes big roads instead of small alleys, and, crossing water, takes boat instead of swimming" (*Da Dai Liji* 52). For this reason, Confucius tells Zengzi that to take care of one's physical body is only the beginning of filial piety, which consummates in establishing a good reputation to illuminate and bring honor to one's parents.

Apparently, Zengzi keeps in mind what Confucius says. Thus, he himself also realizes that "there are three kinds of filial piety. The great one is to bring honor to one's parents, the middle one is not bring dishonor to them, and the small one is to take physical care of them" (*Da Dai Liji* 52). So in addition to taking physical care of one's parents, to be a filial child, one should not do bad things to bring dishonor to one's parents; furthermore, one ought to positively do good things to bring honor to parents. In Zengzi's view, one may make one's parents ashamed or proud of oneself not only by what one does but also by what one says. Thus he says that "hating words are destroyed by a filial person, rumors stop at a filial person, and beautiful words come out of a filial person" (*Da Da Liji* 50). In the *Book of Filial Piety*, it is also claimed that a filial person "does not say anything that is against propriety and does not do anything against moral principles. . . . Thus, even if one's words spread through the whole world, there is never any fault; and even if one's action affects the whole world, there is never any complaint" (*Xiaojing* 4). Moreover, a filial person says and does good things and does not say or do bad things not only when his or her parents are still alive, as a person's filial duty ceases not when his or her parents die but only when he or she dies. Thus, Zengzi states that one ought to be filial until the end of the life and clarifies that "it is not the end of the life of parents but that of oneself" (*Liji* 12.32). In other words, although one's parents, after they die, can no longer be ashamed or proud of what one says or does, what one says or does will still bring either honor or dishonor to them. Thus, "although parents have passed away, considering that doing good things can bring honor to them, one ought to do them resolutely; considering that doing wrong things will bring disgrace to them, one ought to resolutely decide not do to them" (*Liji* 12.17).

It is indeed only in this sense that we can understand Zengzi's otherwise puzzling claim that filial piety includes almost every item of Confucian virtue: "it is not filial to be irreverent in daily life, to be disloyal in serving the ruler, to be not respectful as an official, to be untrustworthy to friends, or to be not courageous in war. . . . Therefore a person of humanity is one who is humane to people through filial piety; a person of moral rightness is one who is morally right through filial piety, a person of loyalty is one who is loyal through filial piety; a person of trustworthiness is trustworthy through filial piety; a person of ritual propriety is ritually appropriate through filial piety; a person who focuses on action practices filial piety; a person with strength is strong in filial piety" (*Da Dai Liji* 52). The reason that filial piety is connected with all these virtues is precisely that parents desire their children to be virtuous, and children's being virtuous brings honor to their parents, while their being vicious brings disgrace to them. Thus an important task of a filial person is to go through self-cultivation to become a virtuous person.

4. Filial piety III: remonstration with parents

In Chinese, the character for filial piety, *xiao* 孝, is often used together with another character for obedience, *shun* 順, to form a two-character phrase, *xiaoshun* 孝順, literally meaning filial obedience or simply obedience to one's parents. It is certainly true that when Confucius talks about filial piety, he does include obedience to one's parents in it. Indeed, according to one interpretation of *Analects* 2.8 discussed above, this is precisely what Confucius means: one ought to know what parents think before they say it and do what they like and don't do what they don't like. This understanding gets further support from *Analects* 1.11: "To observe what your father has in mind when he is alive and observe what your father did after he dies. If you don't change your father's way for three years after he dies, you can be regarded as a filial son."[6]

Thus, Zigong, one of Confucius's students, wants to confirm with Confucius that one's obedience to parents is filial piety, just like a minister's obedience to the king is loyalty. However, Confucius replies, "How shallow you are! You don't understand. In the ancient, when a good king of a big state has seven ministers who dare to remonstrate, the king will not make mistakes; if a middle sized state has five remonstrating ministers, the state will have no danger; if a small state has three remonstrating ministers, the official salaries and positions can last. If a father has a remonstrating child, he will not fall into doing things without propriety; and if a scholar has a remonstrating friend, he will not do immoral things. So how can a son who merely obeys parents be regarded as being filial, and a minister who merely obeys the ruler be regarded as being loyal? To be filial and loyal is to examine what to follow" (*Kongzi Jiayu* 9; 57; the same passage with slight variance also appears in *Xunzi* 29.3).[7]

In this passage, Confucius denies that a filial son ought to be blindly obedient to his parents but emphasizes the importance of remonstration. We ought to obey our parents only about right things, and should not obey when our parents ask us to do wrong things or even when our parents themselves are doing wrong things. Later, Xunzi summarizes that "there are three scenarios in which filial children ought not to obey their parents: (1) if their obedience will endanger their parents, while their disobedience will make their parents safe, then it is truly loyal for filial children to not obey their parents; (2) If obedience will bring disgrace to their parents, while disobedience will bring honor to their parents, then it is moral for filial sons to disobey their parents; (3) if obedience will lead to a life of beast, while disobedience will lead to a civilized life, then it is reverent for filial children to disobey their parents. Therefore, it is not proper for a son to not obey what should be obeyed, and it is not loyal for a child to obey what cannot be obeyed. It is great filial piety to understand when to obey and when not to obey in order to be reverent and respectful, loyal and trustworthy, and act with sincerity and carefulness" (*Xunzi* 29.2).

It is important to point out that in the above passage regarding remonstration, Confucius does not make a distinction between what loyal ministers are supposed to do to their rulers and what filial children are supposed to do to their parents. Just as loyal ministers ought to remonstrate with their rulers, filial children ought to remonstrate with their parents. This contradicts what is said in the *Tan'gong* chapter of the *Book of Rites*, where it is stated that "in serving parents, one ought not to disclose their wrongdoings or to remonstrate with them against wrongdoing. . . . In serving rulers, one ought to remonstrate with them against wrongdoing and disclose their wrongdoings" (*Liji* 3.2). Clearly, this passage does not represent Confucius's view. In this respect, *Analects* 4.18 is the most important and relevant. As it is also subject to different interpretations, we are going to examine it part by part.

The first part is not very controversial. It says, "when serving your parents, [if they are wrong] you ought to gently remonstrate with them." The only scholarly disagreement in interpreting this part is related to the character translated here as "gently," *ji* 幾. While most commentators adopt this interpretation, the Qing Dynasty neo-Confucian Wang Fuzhi 王夫之 (1619–92) claims that it means "at the beginning [of parents' wrongdoing]." So this part of the passage says in effect that children ought to remonstrate at the very beginning of parents' wrongdoing, as when the wrongdoing is fully done, it is difficult to stop (see Cheng Shude: 272). While it is not consequential to the point I make here, I still think it more appropriate to understand the character as "softly" or "gently" when remonstrating. It is taken for granted that one ought to remonstrate before the wrongdoing is committed and not after, or even at the beginning of the wrongdoing being committed, if the purpose of remonstration is to ensure that one's parents do not do immoral things. The question is how one ought to remonstrate. Clearly Confucius does not think that a filial child ought to yell at his or her parents. Instead, as is stated in the *Book of Rites*, "one ought to remonstrate with low tone, nice facial expression, and soft voice" (*Liji* 12.15). While I think this is what *ji* really means, what is important and noncontroversial is that, for Confucius, a filial person does not have to obey his or her parents blindly. Instead he ought to remonstrate with them against wrongdoing.

However, there are more scholarly disagreements on the next part of this *Analects* passage, which I shall translate this way: "when you see your will is not followed by your parents, you ought to remain reverent [toward your parents] and yet not go against [your will]." The controversial part is what I translate as "not go against," *buwei* 不違, which can also be translated as "not disobey," mainly because in the original sentence, the object of this verb, *buwei*, is not explicitly stated. According to a more common understanding, the object of this verb is the same as the object of the verb preceding it, *jing* 敬, here translated as "to be reverent toward." Although the object of this verb is not explicitly stated either, there is no disagreement that it means parents; and since these two verbs are used together, it is natural to think that these two verbs have the same object. Thus, according to this interpretation, this part of the *Analects* passage ought to be understood as, "when you see your will is not followed, you ought to remain reverent toward your parents and not to disobey them." For example, the Han Dynasty classist Zheng Xuan 鄭玄 (127–200) supports this interpretation by citing the following passage from the *Book of Rites*, "in serving their parents, if after remonstrating them three times they still do not listen, then a son or daughter ought to follow them with crying tears" (in Cheng Shude: 270).[8] In other words, while one ought to remonstrate with one's parents against any wrongdoing, if they don't listen, a filial child ought to feel sad but should either let them do it or even follow along.[9]

In contrast, according to the interpretation I adopt here, while the object of the verb *jing*, "be reverent," is obviously "parents," the object of the verb *bu wei*, "do not go against" is not "parents" but "your will" (*zhi* 志) in the first part of the sentence. Moreover, being reverent toward one's parents is conducive to one's continuing attempt to remonstrate with them. By being reverent toward one's parents, the intimate relationship between child and parents can be preserved or enhanced, which is the best occasion for remonstrating with them. In this connection, Zhu Xi makes a very elegant and convincing argument. In his view, "not going against" has a double meaning: "on the one hand, it means to not go against our original will to remonstrate with them *gently*, in order to avoid making our parents angry by yelling at them; on the other hand, it means to not go against our original will to *remonstrate* with them gently, in order to do all that is possible to put our parents in a faultless situation. . . . When our parents do not listen to our initial remonstration, it is wrong for us to stop remonstrating with them in order to avoid making them angry; it is also wrong to remonstrate with them in a way that makes our parents angry" (Zhu 1986: 705).

There are several reasons for adopting our interpretation. First, in the version of the *Analects* used by Huang Kan, the two verbs are connected with a conjunction word, *er* 而 (see Cheng Shude: 270), which has the meaning of "but," indicating a transition between two somewhat opposite meanings: being reverent to parents and yet not going against one's will to remonstrate with them. Second, in another place of the *Analects*, Confucius uses *wu wei* 無違, a synonym to *buwei*, both meaning "not going against." There, Meng Yizi also asks about filial piety, and Confucius replies "*wu wei* (do not go against)." His student Fan Chi asks what this means. While we may all expect Confucius to say "do not go against your parents' will," since he is talking about filial piety, Confucius surprises us by replying that "when your parents are alive, serve them with propriety, and after they die, bury them with propriety and worship them with propriety" (*Analects* 2.5). So what he means by *buwei* is to not go against propriety instead of the will of parents. It would thus be inconsistent if Confucius, in *Analects* 4.18, asks people to not go against the will of their parents.[10] Third, such an interpretation goes well with the last part of the *Analects* passage, which I translate as "you ought not to have complaints even if you wear yourself out by doing so."

In this last part, the key word is *lao* 勞, translated here as "wear yourself out." Song Dynasty classist Xing Bing 邢昺 (932–1010) understands it differently, claiming that it means "being severely hit by parents." Thus, for him, this part of the *Analects* passage means that "even if you are hit severely by your parents for your remonstration, you ought not to have any complaint." This interpretation must have taken into consideration the chapter in the *Book of Rites* that appears to be a paraphrase of *Analects* 4.18. After the sentence about how to remonstrate with parents gently quoted three paragraphs back, it is stated that "if your remonstration is not taken by your parents, you ought to remain reverent and filial. If they are happy, you ought to resume gentle remonstration; if they are not happy, however, instead of letting parents causing harm to neighbors, you ought to use extreme form of remonstration. If at this extreme form of remonstration your parents get angry and unhappy, hitting you hard with whips, you still ought not to complain against them; instead you ought to remain reverent and filial to them" (*Liji* 12.15).

This passage from the *Book of Rites* is consistent with the *Analects* passage as we interpret it. Both insist that, if our remonstration is not taken, rather than letting parents commit wrongdoing or assisting them to do so, we ought not to give up our effort at remonstrating with them. More importantly, it adds that when our continuous *gentle* remonstration does not work and our parents are about to do wrong, we ought to do more than gentle remonstration to stop them from causing harm to neighbors. This may make our parents angry, and they may thus hit us, but we ought not to have any complaint. This is a very interesting point, a point that Confucius may well accept. Still the original *Analects* passage that we have been discussing does not mention our stopping parents from causing harm to neighbors and being hit by our parents because of that. So I agree with most commentators of the *Analects*, who understand the passage to mean that children continue to remonstrate with their parents. For example, according to Huang Kan, "when parents don't listen to our remonstration, we ought to continue to remonstrate with them for tens and even hundreds of times and dare not to withdraw our labor and lodge complaints against our parents." For another example, according to Lü Bogong 呂伯恭, "in order to move parents to a faultless station, we ought to think front and back, left and right, by hook or by crook, exhausting all possible ways. Even though we are thereby exhausted physically and mentally, we ought not to lodge any complaint against our parents" (both in Cheng Shude: 271).

Now we can put the whole passage together. Confucius asks us, when serving our parents, to remonstrate with low tone, appropriate facial expressions, and soft voice, if we are aware that our parents are going to do wrong things. If our parents don't listen to our initial remonstrations, we ought to remain reverent and filial toward them but not change our mind. Instead, we ought to think of all possible ways to dissuade our parents from the wrongdoing, instead of letting them proceed to cause harm to neighbors (see *Liji* 12.15). Even if this process exhausts us physically and mentally, however, we should not make any complaint about our parents.

If this is the case, then how do we understand *Analects* 1.11, quoted at the beginning of this section, in which Confucius says that a filial person ought to know and do what his or her parents think when they are alive and observe what they did after they die without changing their way of doing things for 3 years? The key to understanding this passage is to get clear what Confucius means by the thinking and practice of parents that a filial child is supposed to observe and the way that a filial child is not supposed to change for 3 years after the death of his or parent. Yang Bojun claims that all these mean right things, since if they are bad, Confucius would not think a filial child ought to observe and not change them. However, the question is that, if they are right, they should not be changed even after 3 years. In this context, thus, I agree with Qian Mu, according to whom what Confucius has in mind are ways of running routine family matters, such as the budget for various rituals, gifts to relatives, arrangement of food and cloth for family members, etc., which are more or less morally neutral.

There is no urgency to change even if there are more efficient ways to run them (Qian 2005a: 16). On moral matters, however, if what parents think and do is wrong, then a filial child ought to try to have them changed even when the parents are alive; and if what parents think and do is right, they ought not to be changed at all even after their death.

It is thus clear that, for Confucius, it is important for us to remonstrate with our parents against any possible wrongdoings, which means that we should not blindly obey our parents. Moreover, although we tend to think that filial piety is inseparably connected with obedience to parents, for Confucius, remonstration with parents is an essential component of filial piety. This is already made clear even in the *Analects* passage that we have been analyzing so far, which says that, "in *serving* parents, we ought to remonstrate with them gently." So remonstration is a way to serve our parents. However, in what sense is remonstration with our parents a service to them and therefore a filial action? When we are remonstrating with our parents against any wrongdoing, it appears that we have in mind the interest of the victims of the potential wrongdoings of our parents who would most likely benefit from such wrongdoings. So, apparently, in remonstrating with our parents against any wrongdoings, instead of serving our parents' interest, we are serving the interest of the victims of our parents' potential wrongdoings. Understood this way, we may still consider it to be moral to remonstrate, but in what sense is it a service to our parents and an indication of our filial piety to them?

To fully understand Confucius's view that remonstration is a way to serve our parents and an essential component of our filial piety, let us recall an important point made in Chapter Two: it is in the interest of a person to be virtuous and not in the interest of a person to be vicious. As we have seen, for Confucius, this is not an egoist thesis familiar in the Western philosophical tradition. In this egoistic sense, to be moral, for example, to be honest, is the best policy to serve our interest. First, for example, since it is our self-interest to ensure that other people be honest to us, and it seems that our being honest to them is the most reliable way to win their honesty to us. Second, our being honest to others is also the most reliable way to serve our other interests. For example, if I own a business, to be honest to my customers not only wins their repeated business but also attracts new customers because of my good reputation; either way it serves my interest to make more money. Third, it is much easier to be honest than to be dishonest. To be honest, we only need to tell the truth in every situation. To be dishonest, however, requires us to remember what lies we have previously told and make sure that we do not tell a lie (or conveniently or accidentally tell a truth) that contradicts our previous lies. Since no one's mind is a computer, sooner or later, a dishonest person will be found to be dishonest, which makes it useless for the person to continue to be dishonest. These, however, are obviously not what Confucius means by self-interest in being virtuous.

To understand Confucius's view that it is in one's interest to be virtuous and not in one's interest to be vicious, we must keep in mind not only the Confucian distinction between interest in external well-being and interest in internal well-being but also the Confucian ranking of the latter over the former, as it is our internal well-being that distinguishes us as human beings from other beings. So a filial person, who is supposed to serve the interest of his or her parents, should not only pay attention to their external well-being but also to their internal well-being; moreover, when our parents' external well-being comes into conflict with their internal well-being, to be filial, we ought to pay more attention to their internal well-being. Since parents normally stand to gain externally but to lose internally from their wrongdoings, we ought to remonstrate with them against such wrongdoing, more for the sake of the (internal) interest of our parents than for the sake of the (external) interest of the victims of our parents' potential wrongdoing.

It is thus interesting to see Confucius's contrasting perceptions of two of his students, Zengzi and Min Ziqian 閔子騫. Both are included in the *Complete Pictures of the Twenty Four Exemplars of Filial Piety* (*Quanxiang Ershi Si Xiao* 全相二十四孝), edited by the Yuan Dynasty scholar Guo Jujin 郭居敬 in the form of poetry, later accompanied with pictures, that names the 24 people, starting with the legendary Sage King Shun, with the most moving stories about their filial piety.[11] Zengzi shows his filial piety in both his whole-hearted care of his parents and in his complete obedience to them, as demonstrated by his attitude when his father commits wrongdoing toward him. As we have seen in Chapter Two, Confucius disapproves of Zengzi's blind obedience and asks him to follow the example of the Sage King Shun, who does not let his parents commit wrongdoing toward him. In contrast, Confucius exclaims: "How filial Min Ziqian is indeed! No one can disagree with what his parents and brothers say about him!" (*Analects* 11.5). So what did Min Ziqian do that won him such high praise from Confucius?

Min Ziqian's mother died young, and his father remarried and had two sons with his second wife. Min's stepmother mistreated him but took good care of her own two sons. On a cold winter day, while driving a carriage, Min Ziqian began to shiver and lost hold of the rein. His father got mad and hit him with the whip, which ripped open his coat so that the reed catkins came out. Then his father held the hands of his other two sons who were also in the carriage. Feeling their hands warm, his father checked their coats and found that they were padded with cotton rather than reed catkins. Realizing that his wife had been discriminating against Min Ziqian, he planned to divorce her. Min Ziqian kneeled down, begging his father to forgive his stepmother, saying that "if you keep her, only one of your sons is cold; but if you divorce her, all your three sons will be cold." This is a typical form of the gentle remonstration that Confucius advocates in *Analects* 4.18. Moved by Min Ziqian's selflessness, his father accepted his remonstration and changed his mind. Moreover, his stepmother and stepbrothers were also moved and transformed by it. From then on, his stepmother treated him as she treated her own two sons, and his stepbrothers loved him as an older brother.[12]

5. Why a filial son does not disclose his father's stealing a sheep

Now it is time for us to return to the difficult passage mentioned at the beginning of this chapter: "The governor of She told Confucius, 'in our village, there is an upright person, Zhigong 直躬. When his father stole a sheep, he bore witness against him.' Confucius said, 'in my village, those who are upright are different: father does not disclose his child's wrongdoings, and child does not disclose his father's wrongdoing. Uprightness lies within it'" (*Analects* 13.18).[13] Critics of Confucianism often claim that, since Confucius himself regards honesty and uprightness as important moral virtues, he should praise the son who bears witness against his father stealing a sheep rather than the one who does not disclose his father's wrongdoing. The very fact that he does the opposite shows that Confucius puts family relations, wrongly, above the virtue of honesty and uprightness (Liu 2004: 859). In contrast, defenders of Confucianism often emphasize the importance of the natural and genuine filial love a son feels toward his father, and claims that this is what Confucius means by uprightness. Thus the governor of She and Confucius seem to have two different understandings of uprightness. For the former, uprightness means impartiality: upright persons treat their family members in exactly the same way as they treat other people. They will bear witness against any wrongdoers and so will not do anything differently if the wrongdoers are family members. On the other hand, when Confucius says that uprightness lies in the son's not disclosing his father stealing a sheep, he is referring to the son's "unconcealable genuine feeling" toward his father (Meng 2004: 460; see also Guo 2011a: 6).

So the controversy over this *Analects* passage appears to be one between these two senses of "uprightness," with the one stressing the importance of the natural feeling among family members and the other emphasizing the significance of social justice. Either one, taken by itself, is good, but in this particular case, they come into conflict. It seems that we are facing a dilemma. Defenders of Confucianism take the horn of family feelings. There are a few good reasons for them to do so, none of which, understandably, seems convincing to the critics of Confucianism. For example, it may be argued that for Confucius, family is the basic social unit. Thus to maintain a harmonious family is also to maintain "a rational and ordered society with normal ethical relationships" (Guo 2004: 14). This, however, is not acceptable to critics of Confucianism. For them, even if the mutual nondisclosure of wrongdoings among family members can maintain a harmonious family, which they doubt, it cannot maintain a healthy society: if every family, which has a member who commits a wrongdoing, does it, no wrongdoers will be punished, and potential wrongdoers will be encouraged to commit wrongdoing. The result will be that no justice exists in the society (see Huang 2003: 961).

Another common defense is to use the analogy of family love as the root of a tree and love for others as its branch. This defense is based on *Analects* 1.2: "superior persons pay attention to root, as when the root is established, the Way will grow. Filial piety and brotherly love are the root of [the virtue of] humanity" (*Analects* 1.2). In this analogy, in normal situations, family love and love for others are consistent, as the latter is a natural outgrowth of the former, just like a branch is a natural outgrowth of its root. Thus Mencius says that "if you treat the aged in your family in a way befitting their venerable age, you will be able to extend it to the aged of other families; if you treat the young in your family in a way befitting their tender age, you will be able to extend it to the young of other families" (*Mencius* 1a7). Thus, if the two come into conflict in a particular case, one's love for family members takes precedence over one's love for other human beings, since the former is the root, and the latter its branches. When a branch is cut off, a new branch can grow as long as the root is preserved; however, if the root is cut, then not only can no new branches grow; existing branches will not be able to survive either. This defense, however, also fails to convince critics. For them, just as a healthy branch grows only from a healthy root, moral relationships with people outside one's family can only develop from moral family relationships; just as we must fix the root if it has disease, not only for the sake of the branches growing from it but also for its own sake, we also must correct the problem of a family member, if the member does something wrong, not only for the sake of our relationship with others but also for the sake of the family member himself or herself; and to correct the problem of this family member, it is not right for us to keep it from the public.

Still another defense is based on legal or moral realism, according to which a law or a moral principle cannot require people to do what is not possible for them to do. For example, Fan Zhongxin 范忠信 argues that when we make a law or even establish a moral principle, we must consider the anticipated possibility. Thus, even if a proposed law or moral principle by itself is right, it should not be adopted if what it requires is not something most people can do. He further relates this idea to the issue of the governor of She's praise of Zhigong's bearing witness against his father as being upright, saying that it was and still is not a standard that most of us as human beings can accept (see Fan 2011: 382–3; and Yang 2004: 107–8). This is essentially what Owen Flanagan calls the principle of minimal psychological realism, according to which we need to "make sure when constructing a moral theory or projecting a moral ideal, that the character, decision processing, and behaviour prescribed are possible, or are perceived to be possible for creatures like us" (Flanagan 1991: 34). Clearly this defense cannot convince critics of Confucianism either. Suppose a morality does not require a son to disclose his parents' wrongdoing because it is not something most human beings can do. If Zhigong indeed does it, however, what he does must be praiseworthy, and perhaps more praiseworthy than someone who merely does what morality requires him or her to do, since what Zhigong does in this case is something most people cannot do. While his action is not morally obligatory, it is supererogatory. However, clearly this is not how Confucius looks at what Zhigong does.

While I think that none of these Confucian justifications for taking the horn of family love are convincing to critics, I don't mean that those critics have provided justifications for taking the horn of the broad love for nonfamily members that are convincing to the defenders of Confucianism. We may have to wait patiently for each side to provide justification for the horn it takes of the dilemma that is convincing to the other. Yet I start to suspect that the very notion that this *Analects* passage presents us with a dilemma is perhaps wrong, even though this is also what I once thought (Huang 2007: 6). There are two reasons for my suspicion. First, as I argued in Chapter Two, uprightness for Confucius is not simply to say or do what one truly feels but to say or do what is truly right. More importantly, a central component of Confucius's conception of uprightness is that a person with the virtue of uprightness is not only upright himself or herself but also aims to make nonupright persons upright. If this is the case, Confucius's conception of uprightness is not materially different from the one held by the governor of She. Their disagreement is only about which action, to bear witness against one's father or not disclose his father's wrongdoing, is a better expression of such uprightness.

Second, according to the common conception, Zhigong puts social justice ahead of filial piety, while the person Confucius praises does exactly the opposite. This assumes the dichotomy between filial piety and social justice, at least in this particular case. However, while filial piety means to take care of our parents, as pointed out in the last section of the chapter, to take care of our parents, we need be concerned not only with their external well-being but also with their internal well-being, which requires us to make sure that our parents do not do immoral things and, if already done, they correct themselves. Filial piety in this sense is perfectly consistent with social justice or our love for people outside our family. Thus, to simply not disclose our parents' wrongdoings, which causes harm to their internal well-being in addition to the harm to the external well-being of their victims, may be taken by our parents as our approval of their wrongdoings, which is not only not conducive to the enhancement of their internal well-being but will, in contrast, encourage them to do more wrongdoings and therefore cause further harm to their internal well-being.

If nondisclosure of our parents' wrongdoing itself cannot enhance our parents' internal well-being and consequently the external well-being of those with whom our parents interact, why does Confucius say that uprightness lies within it? And in what sense is our nondisclosure of our parents' wrongdoing a better expression of our uprightness than our bearing witness against our parents' wrongdoing? To understand this, I think that the view of Cai Yuanpei 蔡元培 (1868–1940) that Guo Qiyong brings to our attention is particularly relevant: "if our parents give a command to do a wrong thing, we not only ought to disobey but also ought to remonstrate with them to stop it. If we know that it is a wrong thing to do and yet still do it, even if reluctantly, because it is our parents' command, then not only we ourselves commit a crime but also thereby put our parents in an immoral situation. This is indeed a great lack of filial piety! If our parents have unfortunately committed a wrongdoing, it is also not Confucius's way if we publically disclose it instead of seeking remedies of it secretly. This is what Confucius means by saying that parents don't disclose their children's wrongdoing, and children don't disclose their parents' wrongdoing" (Quoted in Guo 2011: 1).

I think what Cai says here is quite consistent with Confucius's view about remonstration, as a central component of filial piety, examined in the last section. It is thus clear that, after our parents committed a wrongdoing, Confucius thinks that, to be filial, we ought not to disclose it, but we are not supposed to stop here. What is more important is to seek remedies for our parents' wrongdoing, and for Confucius, the value of nondisclosure of our parents' wrongdoings is that it serves to create an atmosphere favorable to such remedies. Cai does not mention explicitly what such remedies are. However, given Confucius's emphasis on the importance of a filial son's persistent and tireless remonstration with parents, we can imagine that it is to remonstrate with our parents to correct themselves. In our discussion of *Analects* 4.18 about remonstration above, we primarily have in mind the situation in which our parents are about to commit wrongdoings, and the purpose of the remonstration is that they change their mind and not commit them; however, if the wrong is already done, then clearly, to be filial, we ought to remonstrate with our parents again so that not only the wrong can be righted, but more importantly our parent can also be made a good person. In this connection, I find Chen Qiaojian 陳乔見 is particularly perceptive in pointing out that, "a Confucian filial son ought to not disclose the fact of his father's stealing a sheep on the one hand and to remonstrate with his father to return the sheep to its original owner on the other. If one remonstration fails, then do it second time, third time, until the goal is reached" (Chen Qiaojian 2011: 455).

As we have seen, in order for the remonstration to be effective, that is, in order for our parents to be willing to listen to our remonstration, Confucius recommends that we ought to remonstrate with them *gently*. If we yell at our parents for their wrongdoings, our parents will naturally get mad, and consequently it is very unlikely that they will listen to our remonstration. So it is important to maintain an intimate atmosphere for remonstration. Now suppose that a son discloses his father's wrongdoing. Since his father is not virtuous yet, he will naturally resent his son. In such an atmosphere, if the son wants to remonstrate with his father, it is very unlikely that the father will listen. It is in this sense that not disclosing our parents' wrongdoing is important for any effective remonstration with them. It aims not only to rectify the wrong done, which is the branch of the problem, but also to rectify the wrongdoer, which is the root of the problem. So even for Confucius, nondisclosure of parents' wrongdoing itself is not upright, but uprightness lies within it, because it is what makes the uprightness possible.

In this chapter, I intentionally translate the Chinese character *yin* 隱 as "not disclosing" instead of "concealing" as is commonly done. This is important. The son simply does not disclose his father's wrongdoing in order to maintain the intimate relationship with his parents, conducive to the remonstration that follows it. However, Confucius does not say that a filial son ought to cover up his father's wrongdoing or to obstruct justice when authorities are investigating the case; nor does he say that the authorities ought not to investigate the case of his father's sheep stealing. This point is made clear by the famous hypothetical case envisioned by Mencius, a case often discussed along with the sheep stealing case. In Mencius's hypothetical case, the father of Sage King Shun kills someone. In Mencius's view, Shun, famous for his filial piety, would not bring this case to the attention of Gaoyao, the minister of justice that Shun himself appointed. Not only ought Gaoyao to arrest Shun's father, but also Shun must not order Gaoyao not to do so (*Mencius* 7a35). Thus, the repeated complaint by critics of Confucianism that Confucianism speaks only from the perspective of the wrongdoer and not that of the victims of the wrongdoer is somewhat misplaced (see Huang 2004: 958–9).

We might think that, thus interpreted, there appears to be some inconsistency in Confucius's view: on the one hand, a son ought not to report his father's wrongdoings or bear witness against his father, and, on the other hand, the authority or the victim ought to investigate and find the wrongdoer. We might think simplistically that if it is right for the son to not disclose his father's wrongdoing, then it must be wrong for the authorities to investigate the case, the purpose or at least the result of which is precisely to make his father's wrongdoing known to others. On the other hand, if it is right for the authority to investigate the father's stealing, then it must be wrong for the son not to report it to an authority or refuse to bear witness against his father. However, in Confucius's view, there is no inconsistency. Although in appearance, what the son does and what the authority does cancel each other out, they actually serve the same or at least overlapping purposes, although from the different social roles they respectively play: to right the wrong done and to prevent future wrongdoings.

It is generally understood that the reason Confucius does not approve Zhigong's bearing witness against his father for stealing a sheep is that he wants to earn a good reputation. This is particularly true in the extended version of this story in *Lü's Spring and Autumn*. In this extended version, after Zhigong reported his father stealing a sheep, the authority was about to punish his father. Zhigong asked to be punished on behalf of his father. When the authority was about to punish him, however, he told the authority: "My father stole a sheep but I reported it: Am I trustworthy? When my father was about to be punished, I volunteered to take the punishment for him: Am I filial? Now if you are going to pun-ish a person who is both trustworthy and filial, is there anyone in the state that does not deserve punishment?" Persuaded, the authority decided to not punish him. After hearing that, Confucius said, "How strange that Zhigong can be regarded as trustworthy! He uses one father to try to earn a name twice" (*Lü's Spring and Autumn*: 261).[14]

However, let us assume that Zhigong reported his father stealing a sheep not because he wanted to earn a good reputation for him-self, but because he sincerely believed that his father was wrong, and that he should treat his father's wrongdoing in the same way as he would treat the wrongdoing of anyone else. Would Confucius then approve of his action? If our analysis is correct, I believe that Confucius would still not approve. After reporting his father's steal-ing a sheep to the authority, Zhigong would not be able to make effective remonstrations with his father even if he still desired to do so. We might want to say that there will then be no need for his remonstration, since now it is the job of the authority to have the wrong righted. However, the only thing that the authority will do is to punish his father. Yet, as Confucius has famously pointed out, while punishment may be able to deter a person from committing the same crime again to some extent, it will not make the person feel shame for it (*Analects* 2.3). In other words, punishment can only restrain a person in terms of what the person can do but can-not make the person virtuous so that the person will not commit any wrongdoing again even if he or she is rewarded for doing so. It is in this context that we can see why not disclosing one's parents' wrongdoing is important: it provides a necessary environment in which a son's effective remonstration with his father becomes pos-sible, and such remonstration is an important way to not merely right the wrong done but also to right the wrongdoer.

Now let us also assume that Zhigong offered to take the punish-ment for his father's wrongdoing sincerely rather than merely to earn a good reputation for being filial, and that the authority actu-ally punished him. Would Confucius approve of his action? I think the answer is a bit ambiguous if Zhigong reported the case to the authority first, as by doing so Zhigong again eliminates an oppor-tunity to remonstrate with his father. However, the answer will be somewhat more affirmative if he did not report the case to the authority, which independently learned about his father stealing a sheep.[15] In this context, the hypothetical example of Shun's father's being a murderer, mentioned above, is also relevant. Since the emperor Shun cannot stop his minister of justice, Gaoyao, from doing the job to arrest his father, Mencius says that what Shun can do is to give up his crown and secretly take his father to the edge of the sea, spending the remainder of his life there with his father (*Mencius* 7a35). Although in this hypothetical case, Shun does not have himself killed for the crime committed by his father, his giving up the crown and going into self-exile can also be regarded as a kind of punishment (see Guo 2011a: 3). By spending the rest of his life with his father at the edge of the sea, he could not only be sure that his father would not commit the same crime again but could also take advantage of the intimate relationship between them to remonstrate his father to make him a good person.[16] Of course, this element is not present in Mencius's original hypothetical case, but it is certainly consistent with Confucius's conception of filial piety that stresses remonstration.

The notion of a son's suffering the punishment for a crime committed by his parents may sound absurd to a Western audience. However, in Confucius's view, it is at least part of what makes a person a filial son. On the one hand, his suffering the punishment can be regarded as a form of remonstration. As parents all wish their children well, when seeing one's child suffer punishment for crimes committed by oneself, the parent will naturally have remorse for the crimes he or she committed and thus become motivated to be a good person. On the other hand, in Confucius's view, as we have seen, one important thing a filial son is supposed to do is to ensure that the parents not cause harm to their own internal well-being by their wrongdoing to others, and so the very fact that one's parent does so shows that the son has not fulfilled his filial responsibility. Thus when the son takes the punishment for the crime committed by his parent, the son would also regard it as a punishment for his own failure to fulfill the filial responsibility.

Zheng Jiadong 鄭家棟 points out that a common problem with Confucius's view about not disclosing one's father's stealing a sheep and Mencius's view about Shun's carrying his father to a remote area is that the criminal is still at large, and justice is not done (Zheng 2004: 488). This is also a concern shared by almost all critics of Confucianism. About the former, it is indeed true that the person who committed the crime is still at large. However, in both cases, a suitable environment for remonstration is created to rectify the criminal at large. As a result, the criminal at large will no longer be a criminal. Regarding the latter, of course the authority may want to serve an additional but what seems to me a morally ambiguous purpose: by punishing the wrongdoer, on the one hand, justice is done in the sense that the same degree of the harm is returned to the wrongdoer as the latter inflicted upon the victims, and on the other, potential wrongdoers may be deterred from committing the same wrongdoings. The reason I say that it is a morally ambiguous purpose is that, on the one hand, it is wrong, at least according to the utilitarian theory of punishment, to punish a wrongdoer if the wrongdoer will never commit the same or similar wrongdoing again; and on the other hand, it is wrong, at least according to the retributive theory of punishment, for the authority to use the wrongdoer as a tool to deter other potential wrongdoers. Of course, this involves the central issue of the debate between utilitarian and retributive conceptions of justice in punishment. As this issue seems to be unsolvable, I prefer the restorative conception of justice as alternative: when we identify a wrongdoer, the appropriate or just thing to do is not to inflict the same amount of harm upon this wrongdoer that was inflicted upon the victims to maintain a balance (the retributive conception) or to inflict more harm to the wrongdoer than was inflicted as a deterrent (utilitarian conception). Rather it is to restore this person's internal well-being so that he or she would not have the inclination to commit wrongdoing again (see Huang 2007: 9–12).[17] This justice can be best served by Confucius's suggestion of mutual nondisclosure of wrongdoings among family members, followed by gentle but persistent remonstration.

6. Conclusion

Among his teachings, Confucius's conception of filial piety is one that has been subjected to most severe criticisms and is also one that Western audiences find most difficult to accept: why ought we always obey our parents? Our discussion above shows that this is largely due to a misunderstanding. Confucius's filial piety does include our filial duty to serve our parents with respect and deep love, which is not controversial at all. Yet it also includes two other important aspects, which have often been neglected. The first is that a filial person ought first of all to be a virtuous person. Parents normally all wish their children well, not only physically and mentally, but also morally. This can be seen from the fact that no parents will be upset by their children's being virtuous or are proud of their children's being vicious. Thus any of their children's moral deeds will bring honor to them, while any of their immoral deeds bring disgrace. A filial child thus ought to do things that bring honor to their parents and avoid doing things that bring dishonor. The second is that while a filial person, by definition, ought to take care of his or her parents, for Confucius, this not only includes parents' external well-being but more importantly their internal well-being. Thus it is extremely important for filial children to do all that they can to make sure that their parents do not commit wrongdoings that will cause damage not only to the external well-being of the victims of their wrongdoings but also to their own internal well-being. In Confucius's view, the best way for a filial son or daughter to accomplish this is to remonstrate gently with parents against any wrongdoing if it is not yet done and for righting the wrong if already done. It is indeed in this context that we can understand Confucius's otherwise puzzling view that an upright son ought not to disclose his father stealing a sheep. Here, while nondisclosure of parents' wrongdoing is not an indication of the son's uprightness, it creates or preserves the intimate family atmosphere in which remonstration can most effectively proceed. It is in this sense that Confucius says that the son's uprightness lies in his nondisclosure of the parents' wrongdoing.

NOTES

Chapter Two

1 According to the common interpretation, Weisheng should simply say honestly that he does not have any vinegar. However, I think Confucius's main problem with Weisheng is that he does not say that the vinegar is not his but rather his neighbor's. Rather than sending the person away by simply telling the truth (that he does not have vinegar), perhaps Confucius would approve Weisheng's action if he did not cover up the fact that the vinegar came from his neighbor.

2 In another place, Confucius contrasts three types of people who are good to make friends with, one of whom is an upright person, with three types of people who are bad to make friends with, one of whom is the one who flatters (*Analects* 16.4). So an upright person does not flatter people.

3 In another place, Confucius was recorded as saying: "in the past, those who made strong remonstrations ceased when they died. There has never been one like Shi Yu who, after death, remonstrated with his corps. His loyalty transformed his ruler. How can it be not regarded as uprightness?" (*Kongzi Jiayu* 22; 145).

4 At least this is how Reinhold Niebuhr sees it: "Jesus did not counsel his disciples to forgive seventy times seven in order that they might convert their enemies or make them more favorably disposed. He counseled it as an effort to approximate complete moral perfection, the perfection of God. He did not ask his followers to go the second mile in the hope that those who had impressed them into service would relent and give them freedom. He did not say that the enemy ought to be loved so that he would cease to be an enemy. He did not dwell upon the social consequences of these moral actions, because he viewed them from an inner and a transcendent perspective" (Niebuhr 1960: 263–4).

5 This seems to be what Laozi believes. He not only asks us to "repay injury with a good turn" (*Daodejing* 63) but also explains his reason: "I treat those who are good with goodness, and I also treat those who are not good with goodness. Thus goodness is attained. I am honest to those who are honest, and I am also honest to those who are not honest. Thus honest is attained" (*Daodejing* 49).

6 It might be said that simply avoiding being harmed by a wrongdoer contributes nothing to make the wrongdoer cease to be a wrongdoer. After all, a person can become a wrongdoer not only through a successful wrongdoing but also through intent to commit the wrongdoing. To this, a Confucian can at least have two responses. First, just as a person becomes a virtuous person by doing virtuous things, as stated by Aristotle, a person becomes a vicious person also by doing vicious things. So by eliminating or not providing opportunities for a wrongdoer to commit wrongdoings, we reduce the opportunities for the wrongdoer to become a vicious person. Second, to not allow a wrongdoer to commit wrongdoing is indeed only an initial but also a necessary step to make the wrongdoer cease to be a wrongdoer, a step that has to be followed by other steps, which I shall discuss in Chapter Four.

7 For a more extensive discussion of the problem of Aristotle's function argument, see Huang 2011.

8 In this relation, Xunzi says that the reason people abandoned wicked kings Jie and Zhou and rushed to sage kings Tang and Wu is that, while the former did what people disliked, the latter did what people desired. Then he explains: "What people dislike? They dislike baseness and recklessness, contention and aggression, and a rapacious appetite for profit. What people love? They love ritual propriety and moral rightness, courtesy and deference, and loyalty and trustworthiness" (*Xunzi* 16.4).

9 Thomas Aquinas developed an idea of fraternal correction, "to apply a remedy to the sin considered as an evil of the sinner himself," which is "the same as to procure his good, and procure a person's good is an act of charity, by which we do our friend well" (Aquinas 1952: II-II, q.33, a.1). More importantly, Aquinas thinks that fraternal correction is a kind of spiritual almsdeed, which is more excellent than the corporeal one (Aquinas 1952: II-II, q.32, a.4). Clearly Aquinas's virtue ethics can thus well avoid the self-centeredness objection. However, at least two things deserve our attention. First, Aquinas regards fraternal correction as a virtue of charity, which belongs to the third category of virtue, theological ones, which "can be in us neither naturally, nor through acquisition by the natural powers, but by the infusion of the Holy Spirit" (Aquinas 1952: II-II, q.24, a.2). Second, even though Aquinas does think a virtuous person, out of charity, should be concerned about others' virtues, he still thinks that "a man ought, out of charity, to love himself more than he loves any other person," and "a man ought not to give way to any evil of sin which counteracts his share of happiness, not even that he may free his neighbor from sin" (Aquinas 1952: II-II, q.26, a.5).

10 Thus Aristotle states, "since we say that the good man will resign goods in the way of utility to his friend, he will be loving his friend more than himself. Yes, but his resignation of such goods implies that he is compassing the noble for himself in resigning these to his friend. In a way, therefore, he is loving his friend more than himself, and in a way he is loving himself

most. In respect of the useful he is loving his friend, but in respect of the noble and the good he is loving himself most" (Aristotle: 1212b12–17).

11 In a recent article, Yang Guorong also incidentally endorses this interpretation (Yang Guorong 2011: 49). This interpretation does have support from the *Mencius*, where it is stated that "*zhong* is to teach others to be good" (*Mencius* 3a4), which is based on an *Analects* passage, where Confucius says that if you are *zhong* toward a person, how can you not teach the person? (*Analects* 14.7).

12 Here I adopt the interpretation of this passage by Cheng Yi and Zhu Xi (see Zhu 1986: 645) which, while different from the classical interpretation, is closer to what Confucius says. According to the classical interpretation adopted by a number of interpreters, what Confucius says here is that a virtuous person loves what people love and hates what people hate (see Cheng Shude 1990: 230). The idea is very much to my taste, as it is what I have advocated as the moral copper rule (see Huang 2005), as ethics of difference (see Huang 2010b), and as patient-centered relativism (see Huang 2012), but it is difficult to discern this idea from Confucius's original saying.

13 This is similar to what Aristotle says: "those who are not angry at the thing they should be angry at are thought to be fools, and so are those who are not angry in the right way, at the right time, or with the right persons" (Aristotle 1126a5–6).

Chapter Three

1 Aristotle (and, in a slightly different way, Plato) also argues that to be moral is distinctive of being human, but he does not think it is the best thing that humans can and should do. The latter is philosophical contemplation, which, on the one hand, not everyone can do and, on the other hand, may be in conflict with one's being moral, as to be moral one will be busy involving oneself with affairs of other people, while philosophical contemplation needs leisure. I have an expanded discussion of this Aristotelian view and its difference from the Confucian view as presented in this chapter (see Huang 2008: 342–6).

2 In this respect, Mencius makes a series of important analogical arguments. He describes the immoral person as one who abandons a comfortable home and proper road (the virtue of humanity) (*Mencius* 4a10), as one who cares to look for his or her chickens or dogs when lost but not so for his or her own lost heart/mind (*Mencius* 6a11), as one who knows that trees need be taken care of but not that his or her own person need be taken care of (*Mencius* 6a13), as one who cares about his or her finger more than his or her heart/mind (*Mencius* 6a12); and as one who cannot recognize the hierarchical values of the great body (heart/mind) and small (physical) body (*Mencius* 6a14).

3 For example, Meng Peiyuan 蒙培元, in his interpretation of the relationship between "realization of oneself" (*zi cheng* 自成) and "realization of others" (*cheng wu* 成物) in a passage from the *Doctrine of Mean*, claims that "'realization of oneself' is the starting point, while 'realization of others' is the result. The key to the learning of sage is 'realization of oneself.' 'Realization of others can take place only after one realizes oneself'" (Meng 1993: 18). As we have seen, this cannot be correct. One cannot realize oneself without at the same time realizing others, as *cheng wu* is an inherent part, perhaps even the very definition, of *cheng ji*.

4 It has to be pointed out that, in the commentary history of the *Analects*, there are two major different interpretations of this passage, largely related to the two different interpretations of the term *gu* 固, translated here as "inflexible." The interpretation adopted here is one of them. The other interpretation is based on another basic meaning of the term *gu* as "being solid." According to this interpretation, what we have here is merely a phrase and not a complete sentence, and it has to be understood in connection with what appears in front of it in the passage, which as a whole then means that "if one lacks reverence, one will not inspire awe and one's learning will not be solid" (see Cheng Shude 1990: 33–4). I think Chen Daqi 陳大齊 (1886–1983) has made a convincing argument, by examining other appearances of the same Chinese character *gu* in the *Analects* and analyzing the function of learning in other *Analects* passages, that the interpretation adopted here is better (see Chen Daqi 1969: 6–8).

5 The idea that everyone has the ability to become virtuous or even be a sage is also very much emphasized by Mencius, who claims that "all you need to do is to make the effort. The problem is not that people do not have sufficient strength, but that they refuse to make the effort" (*Mencius* 6b2). Thus, he makes the famous distinction between "unable" (*buneng* 不能) and "unwilling" (*buwei* 不為). Anyone who is immoral is immoral not because he or she is unable to be moral but because the person is unwilling to be moral. While there are things that humans are unable to do, such as "striding over the North Sea with Mount Tai under one's arm" (*Mencius* 1a7), to be moral is not one of them. To say that one cannot do moral things is like saying that one cannot lift a feather or one cannot see a cartload of firewood, as he explains to King Xuan of Qi (*Mencius* 1a7).

Chapter Four

1 Before Confucius, Shuxiang 叔向 in the state of Jin 晉 was also a private teacher; around the time of Confucius, Deng Xi 鄧析 in the state of Zheng 鄭, Shao Zhengmao 少正卯 in the State of Lu 魯, Laozi 老子 in the royal court of Zhou 周, Ju Boyu 蘧伯玉 in the state of Wei 衛, Yan Yin 晏嬰 in the state of Qi 齊, Laolaizi 老萊子 in the state of Chu 楚, Zichan 子產 in the state of Zheng 鄭, and Meng Gongchuo 孟公綽 in the state of Lu 魯 all taught students in their unofficial positions (see Cai Shangsi 1982: 177–8).

2 While the most stupid cannot be made wise through education, the most wise are supposed to be born with knowledge and have no need of education.

3 In *Analects* 16.9, Confucius ranks this type of people at the bottom. Above are three better groups of people, those who learn after being vexed with difficulties, those who know by learning, and those who are born with knowledge.

4 In one of the bamboo strips excavated at Guodian 郭店, *Zun Deyi* 尊德義 (*Respecting Virtue and Rightness*)—which some scholars speculate may have been written around Confucius's time—there is a related statement: "People may not be deluded" (strip no. 31, in Jingmen 1998: 174).

5 Because the phrase "the master says" does not appear in front of this passage as it does in most other passages, some commentators believe this saying is from one of Confucius's students. Other commentators claim that this continues with the previous passage, which starts with the phrase "the master says," and so believe that this is also a saying by Confucius (see Cheng Shude 1990: 742–4). The first group of commentators thus separates this passage from the previous one and numbers it as *Analects* 11.3, while the second group combines it with the previous one as part of *Analects* 11.2. Since classical Chinese does not have punctuation marks, no easy verdict can be made on this issue.

6 On these four subjects as all subjects of moral education, Qian Mu, an important contemporary intellectual historian, comments that "virtuous conduct is listed as the first subject, but this does not mean that virtuous conduct excludes language, government, and literature and is something other than the three. . . . In terms of virtuous conduct, other three are its branches and belong to virtuous conduct. . . . Literature also includes the other three, as other three have all originated from the classics" (Qian Mu 2005: 278).

7 Zhu Xi regards the first two as literature, *wen* 文, and the other four as techniques, *shu* 術; see Cheng Shude 1990: 444.

8 This is the only place where Confucius talks about charioteeing in the *Analects*. There are several other discussions of archery. In 3.7, Confucius mentions it when he claims that there is no contention among superior persons: "even in archery, they bow and yield to one another as they go up and drink together after they go down"; in 3.16, he says that "people's strength varies, and the point of archery is not to pierce through the hide"; and 7.27 is a student's report of Confucius not shooting at roosting birds.

9 Cai Shangsi argues that the six arts can be divided into three categories: "calligraphy and mathematics are basic knowledge of literacy. Ritual and music are basic knowledge needed for political and religious activities of the nobles; and archery and charioteering are main skills in military activities" (Cai 1982: 175).

10 Kuang Yaming goes even further. Having in mind the communist education system in contemporary China, Kuang claims that Confucius's education also includes the three aspects, moral education (*de* 德), intellectual education (*zhi* 智), and physical education (*ti* 體), and argues that

charioteering and archery belong to physical education (see Kuang 1990: 307).

11 Chen Daqi argues that "Confucius' philosophy of education is based on moral philosophy, and therefore the goal of its education is the ideal person, and its focus is on personal cultivation. Confucius's ideal person is the superior person (*junzi*), and so the goal of his education is the education of the superior person" (Chen Daqi 1964: 273).

12 Thus, it should be clear that while to be a superior person is not to acquire specific skills, a superior person often does desire to have many skills. This can explain a relevant passage: "A superior person is troubled by his or her own lack of ability and not by others' failure to recognize it" (*Analects* 15.19; see also 14.30). Chen Daqi uses this passage to show that having many skills is a necessary qualification for one to be a superior person (Chen 1969: 172). However, it is important to see that, in this passage, Confucius is concerned about what a superior person should be troubled with, one's own lack of abilities or other people's lack of knowledge about one's having abilities, and not about what makes one a superior person: to have abilities or to have virtues. While a superior person can, desires to, and often does, have many skills, the person is a superior person not because he or she has many skills but because the person has virtues. For example, a superior person loves his or her parents, which is knowledge as virtue; but in order to find the best way to love his or her parents, the person must learn some technical skills (to keep them warm in the winter and cool in the summer, for example). However, a person who lacks such technical skills due to limited inborn intelligence is not less filial than the one who has them.

13 It is in this sense that, for Chen Lai, "although we cannot simply claim that indeed 'virtue can be taught,' we can state emphatically that virtue can be learned.. . . Thus, in answer to Socrates' and Plato's question of whether virtue can be taught, the ancient Confucians would be inclined to rephrase the question as 'Can virtue be learned?' as a way of expressing the Confucian problematic" (Chen Lai: 319). Virtue can of course be learned for Confucius, but our question here is a harder one: whether virtue can also be taught for Confucius.

14 Kupperman also recognizes the importance for Confucius of teaching by example and thinks that "this is one of the reasons that Confucius recommends that you avoid friendships with people who are not equal to you (*Analects* 1.8). Within a nuclear family this especially points toward the importance of parents' behavior, which constitutes crucial role-modeling in early life. They set the tone in the child's life. If there is anything at all to the view that role models are important in people's moral development, then the quality of these early personal relations within a family is likely to matter considerably" (Kupperman 2010: 19).

15 The character translated here as "the multitude" is *shi* 師, which literally means one's teacher. My translation follows the Qing dynasty scholar Huang Shisan's 黃式三 interpretation (in Cheng Shude 1990: 1124). Contemporary scholar Qian Mu 錢穆 also adopts this interpretation, saying

that, although teacher and student are living in the same period, after a student graduates, the teacher normally is not next to him or her, and so it should not be understood as "yielding to teachers" (Qian 2005: 422).

16 For an excellent discussion of being morally moved, see Wang 2010.

17 *Kongzi Jiayu* records a more detailed discussion by Confucius: "The more those in higher positions revere their parents, the more those in lower positions will practice filial piety; the more those in higher positions respect their older brothers, the more those in lower positions will practice brotherly love; the more charitable those in higher positions are, the more generous those in lower positions will become; the more those in higher positions maintain a close relationship with worthy people, the more those in lower positions will choose good people as friends; the more those in higher positions love morality, the less likely those in lower positions will hide their moral deficiency; the more those in higher positions dislike greed, the more those in lower positions will feel it shameful to compete for benefit; the more deferential those in higher positions are, the more shame those in low positions will feel for being impolite. These seven teachings are the foundations of governing people. . . . Those in higher positions are exemplars of those in lower positions. When the exemplars are rectified, who else will not be rectified?" (*Kongzi Jiayu* 3; 20).

18 This four-Chinese-character phrase has since become an idiom commonly used to describe the appropriate attitude we should have when a person is caught in wrongdoing.

Chapter Five

1 The debate was initiated by a series of articles by Liu Qingping 劉清平, criticizing Confucius's view as expressed in this passage, along with Mencius's view expressed in *Mencius* 7a35 and 5a3, as a source of corruption in Chinese society, past and present. Guo Qiyong 郭齊勇 published a number of articles defending Confucius's view against Liu's criticism. A few others also joined the debate on both sides. These articles, together with a few related ones, are collected in Guo (ed.) 2004. I edited a special issue of *Contemporary Chinese Thought* (volume 39 [2007], no.1), including some abbreviated English translations of selected articles mostly collected in Guo 2004, together with an Introduction written by myself. I also arranged a symposium discussion on this topic in several issues of *Dao: A Journal of Comparative Philosophy*, starting with an article each by Liu and Guo, presenting their most representative views on this debate (*Dao* 6 [2007].1: 1–37), followed by a number of critical comments by primarily Western scholars (*Dao* 7 [2008].1: 1–55 and 7 [2008].2: 119–174), and concluded with a response each from Liu and Guo (*Dao* 7 [2008].3: 307–324). More recently, one of Guo's former colleagues, Deng Xiaomeng 鄧曉芒, published a series of articles defending Liu against the criticisms by others. These articles are now collected in Deng 2010. Guo and others' responses to Deng are collected in Guo (ed.) 2011.

2 The fourth and the fifth are related to the sense of filial piety to be discussed in the next section.

3 Ye Jingzhu 葉經柱 surmises that the reason Confucius thinks so is perhaps that in his time, most people did take care of their parents' physical needs; however, by Mencius's time, most people did not, which is why Mencius places such emphasis on taking care of parents' physical needs (see Ye 1977: 52).

4 For example, it is claimed, in *On Salt and Iron*, that "to serve one's parents according to their will is the highest filial piety, to serve one's parents with appropriate facial expressions is the second best filial piety, while to merely provide the physical care is the lowest filial piety" (in Cheng Shude: 87).

5 Working from a very different context, Rosalind Hursthouse also points out that not only, in bringing up our children, do we prepare them for life and begin their moral education, but also, when doing so, good parents have their children's interest at heart. Moreover, "having their children's interest at heart, it does not occur to most of them to bring them up to be entirely self-interested and immoral. On the contrary, they see the natural childish impulses to self-gratification and self-indulgence as impulses that need to be modified and redirected, and their natural impulses to love and generosity and fairness as impulses that need to be developed" (Hursthouse 1999: 175).

6 There is disagreement about how to understand the first part of the passage. Here I adopt the interpretation that understands the subject of the verb "observe" (*guan* 觀) to be the son, while what is being observed is the father's thinking and action. According to another interpretation, developed by Kong Anguo 孔安國 (156–74 BCE) and adopted by Zhu Xi, what is being observed is the son's thinking and action, while the subject of the verb "observe" becomes a third party (see Cheng Shude: 43–44). D. C. Lau, in his English translation of the *Analects*, also adopts this interpretation and translates this part as: "Observe what a man has in mind to do when his father is living, and then observe what he does when his father is dead" (Lau: 60). Chen Daqi compares these two interpretations and concludes that the interpretation adopted in this chapter is more plausible (see Chen Daqi 1969: 10–12).

7 In the *Book of Filial Piety*, there is a similar passage. Zengzi says: "I have already heard from you about loving parents, respecting parents, comforting parents, and establishing a good reputation [to illuminate parents]. Now I would like to ask you, my master, whether it is also filial to obey parents." Confucius says, "How can that be? How can that be? In the ancient, an emperor with seven remonstrating ministers would not lose the empire, even if the Way was not prevailing; a duke with five remonstrating ministers would not lose the state, even if the Way was not prevailing; a hereditary official with three remonstrating ministers would not lose his land, even if the Way was not prevailing; a scholar with remonstrating friends would be able to maintain a good reputation; a father with remonstrating children would not fall into immorality (*bu yi* 不義). So when something is not right, then sons and daughters cannot not remonstrate with their fathers, and ministers cannot not remonstrate with their ruler. One ought to remonstrate whenever there is something immoral. How can obedience be regarded as filial piety?" (*Xiaojing* 15).

8 Zheng Xuan indicates that this passage is in the chapter on "Family Rules" (*neize* 內則) of the *Book of Rites*. However, we cannot find this passage in this chapter, chapter 12 in this extant edition. Instead we find it in the second chapter (*Liji* 2.28).

9 This seems to be indeed the view of Zengzi: "if one's parents commit to wrongdoing, one ought to remonstrate and yet not to disobey" (*Da Dai Liji* 52); and "if what parents do conforms to the Way, one ought to follow; if what they do does not conform to the Way, one ought to remonstrate. If one's remonstration is not taken, one ought just to do what parents do as if it is one's own idea. It is not filial to obey parents without remonstration, nor is it filial to remonstrate without obeying parents [if they don't listen]. A filial son's remonstration aims at goodness and therefore should be done without quarrels with parents, as quarrels are the source of disorder" (*Da Dai Liji* 53). However, as we have shown in Chapter Two, Zengzi was criticized by Confucius for being too blindly obedient to his parents even when they are wrong, which actually causes harm to them.

10 Guo Qiyong thus argues that here it also means to not go against rules of propriety (Guo 2011a: 8). Although this is not the interpretation I adopt here, the outcome is the same.

11 Zilu, another student, was also included in the 24 exemplars of filial piety. He grew up in a poor family. When young, while often eating wild vegetable himself, he travelled more than 100 miles to carry rice for his parents. By the time he became an official and had delicious things to eat, his parents had died. He often thought of his parents, saying that "today, even if I would rather eat wild vegetable and take a long way to carry rice for my parents, I could not do that." Having heard that, Confucius praised Zilu, saying that "Zilu served his parents with his whole body when they were alive and with his whole heart after they died" (*Kongzi Jiayu*).

12 This story has multiple dimensions. As the Qing Dynasty scholar Jiao Xun 焦循 (1763–1820) points out, on the one hand, "Min Ziqian remonstrated with his father so that his stepmother would not be thrown out. This was his serving his parents above. [On the other hand,] he didn't have complaints about his two brothers being kept warm while he was left cold and was instead concerned about their being left cold should his stepmother be thrown out. This was his loving his brothers below.... [Originally] the stepmother's cruelty [toward Min Ziqian] was blamable, the two stepbrothers' exclusive enjoyment of warm coats was blamable, and the father's negligence of his wife's discrimination against Min Ziqian was also blamable. However, the whole family was moved and transformed by Min Ziqian's one remonstration, so that the parents didn't lose their kindness to children, and the two brothers didn't lose their brotherly love (*ti* 悌) for Min Ziqian, and what was blamable was made blameless" (in Cheng Shude: 748).

13 The Chinese character that is translated here as stealing is *rang* 攘. According to some commentators, it does not mean the positive action of stealing but simply to keep or not return. So in the *Analects* passage,

it means that the father simply took a lost sheep without attempting to find its original owner (see Guo 2011: 2). This interpretation is perhaps interesting and possibly authentic (although there is also disagreement among classical commentators) but not consequential to our argument. Should one's father indeed take the active action of stealing a sheep, Confucius's view about what a filial son ought to do would not be any different.

14 It is possible that the story does not stop here. According to *Hanfeizi*, the result is that Zhigong was eventually punished, not for his uprightness toward the king but his crookedness toward his father. According to the Qing Dynasty scholar Song Xiangfeng 宋翔鳳, the reason that there is discrepancy between *Hanfeizi* and *Lü's Spring and Autumn*, with the former saying that Zhigong was punished and the latter not, is that, having heard what Confucius said, the authority decided to have Zhigong punished (in Cheng Shude: 924).

15 Zheng Jiadong brought to our attention the story of a son's bearing punishment on his father's behalf as recorded in the *Records of History* (*Shiji* 史記). Shi She 石奢, the prime minister of King Zhao 昭 of Chu 楚, was a person with strength, uprightness, honesty, and integrity, never flattering people nor being afraid of anything in carrying out his duties. Once on a journey within his jurisdiction, there happened to be a murderer. He chased the murderer, only to find out that it was his father. He let his father go and put himself in jail instead. Then he sent someone to tell King Zhao, "the murderer is my father. If I administrate the government by killing my father, I am not filial to him; if I encourage crimes by abolishing laws, I am not loyal to you. Therefore I deserve the death punishment." Perhaps moved by both Shi's filiality and loyalty, King Zhao was not willing to punish him. Shi said, "If I'm not partial to my father, I will not be a filial son; if I don't abide by the laws made by king, I will not be a loyal minister. It is your grace to forgive my crime, but it is my responsibility to receive the punishment and die." Thus he killed himself (Sima 2008b; see Zheng 2004: 487).

16 One related objection to Mencius's view about what Shun ought to do is that, by giving up his crown, Shun abandoned his people (see Liu: 869). However, since part of what it means to be a filial son is to take care of his parents' internal well-being, and since Shun's father committed murder, which not only caused the greatest harm to the external well-being of the victim but also the greatest harm to the internal well-being of Shun's father himself, Shun might consider that he did not do his filial duty well. Since in the Confucian tradition, one cannot be a good ruler without being a good son, Shun might also think that he was no longer qualified to be emperor.

17 This view of Confucius seems to be very different from what is called "putting one's [criminal] family member to death in order to promote greater justice" (*dayi mie qin* 大義滅親) practiced by notable people, the most famous of whom is Bao Zheng 包拯 (999–1062), who, as a judge, put

to death his own nephew as criminal. Since Bao Zheng has been praised throughout history as an exemplary official with absolute impartiality, if Confucius holds a view different from his, at least some justification is needed (see Mu 2004: 967). On this issue, I think Guo Qiyong and Gong Jianping have made a very elegant argument. In their view, however others look at what he did, Bao Zheng himself "must have a deep sense of guilt and regret, as he would realize that he failed to educate his nephew or at least failed to educate him appropriately [as otherwise he would not commit the crime], that he failed to learn [and therefore stop] what his nephew was going to do so that he would not become a criminal, and that he was trying to govern the state while he even failed to govern his own family" (Guo and Gong 2004: 55). What Guo and Gong say here is perfectly consistent with the notion of "moral residue" or "moral remainder" that I discussed in Chapter Four.

REFERENCES

Analects. 1980. In *Translation and Annotation of the* Analects 論語譯注, by Yang Bojun. Beijing: Zhonghua Shuju.

Aquinas, Thomas. 1952. "The Summa Theologica." In *Great Books of the Western World*, vols 19–20. Chicago: Encyclopedia Britannica.

Aristotle. 1963. "Ethica Nicomachea," trans. by W. D. Ross. In *The Works of Aristotle*, vol. 9. Oxford: Oxford University Press.

Bertram, B. C. R. 1976. "Kin Selection in Lions and in Evolution." In *Growing Points in Ethology*, edited by P. P. G. Bateson and R. A. Hinde. Cambridge: Cambridge University Press, pp. 281–302.

Bradley, F. H. 1935. *Ethical Studies*. Oxford: Oxford University Press.

Cai, Shangsi 蔡尚思. 1982. *Confucius' System of Thought* 孔子思想體系. Shanghai: Shanghai Renmin Chubanshe.

Cai, Yuanpei 蔡元培. 1999. *Two Essays on Civic Education* 國民教育二種. Shanghai: Shanghai Wenyu Chubanshe.

Chen, Daqi 陳大奇. 1964. *Confucius's Thoughts* 孔子學說. Taibei: Zhengzhong Shuju.

—1969. *A Tentative Interpretation of the* Analects 論語臆解. Taibei: Shangwu Yinshuguan.

Chen, Lai. 2008. "The Ideal of 'Educating' and 'Learning' in Confucian Thought." In *Educations and Their Purposes*, edited by Roger T. Ames and Peter Hershock. Honolulu: University of Hawaii Press, pp. 310–326.

Chen, Qiaojian 陳乔見. 2011. "The Private and the Public: Self Rule and Rule by Law 私与公：自治与法治." In *Critiques of* A New Critique of Confucian Ethics 《儒家倫理新批判》之批判, edited by Guo Qiyong. Wuhan: Wuhan University Press, pp. 447–492.

Cheng, Hao 程顥, and Cheng Yi 程頤. 1989. *Collected Works of Cheng Brothers* 二程集. Beijing: Zhonghua Shuju 中華書局.

Cheng, Shude 程樹德. 1990. *Collected Commentaries on the* Analects 論語集釋. Beijing: Zhonghua Shuju.

Cohen, G. A. 2002. *If You're an Egalitarian, How Come You're So Rich?* Cambridge, MA: Harvard University Press.

Copp, David. 1997. "The Ring of Gyges: Overridingness and the Unity of Reason." *Social Philosophy and Policy* 14: 86–106.

Da Dai Liji 大戴禮記 (*The Senior Dai's Book of Rites*). 2008. In *The Collected Annotations and Interpretation of the* Senior Dai's Book of Rites 大戴禮記匯校集釋, by Fang Xiangdong 方向東. Beijing: Zhonghua Shuju.

Daxue 大學 (*The Great Learning*). 1994. In *Collected Commentaries on the Four Books* 四書章句集註, by Zhu Xi. Taibei: Da'an Chubanshe.

de Bary, Wm. Theodore. 2011. "Xunzi" (an unpublished paper presented at Columbia University Seminar on Neo-Confucian Studies, November, 2011).

Deng, Xiaomang 鄧曉芒. 2010. *A New Critique of Confucian Ethics* 儒家倫理新批判. Chongqing: Chongqing University Press.

Fan, Zhongxin 范忠信. 2011. "'Anticipated Possibility' and the Legal Orientation toward Sages and Worthies of the Criminal Laws in Our Country '期待之可能性'與我國刑事法的'法治聖賢定位'." In *Critiques of A New Critique of Confucian Ethics*《儒家倫理新批判》之批判, edited by Guo Qiyong. Wuhan: Wuhan University Press, pp. 380–386.

Flanagan, Owen. 1991. *Varieties of Moral Personality: Ethics and Psychological Realism*. Cambridge, MA: Harvard University Press.

Foot, Philippa. 1978. *Virtues and Vices*. Berkeley and Los Angeles: University of California Press.

Great Learning, The. 1963. In *A Source Book in Chinese Philosophy*, trans. and compiled by Wing-Tsit Chan. Princeton: Princeton University Press (translation modified).

Guo, Qiyong 郭齊勇. 2004. "Also on the Mutual Non-disclosure of Wrongdoing between Father and Son and Mencius's Case of Shun." In *A Collection of Essays in the Debate on Confucius Ethics* 儒家倫理爭鳴集, edited by Guo Qiyong 郭齊勇. Wuhan: Hubei Jiaoyu Chubanshe, pp. 12–20.

—2011. "Introduction." In *Critiques of A New Critique of Confucian Ethics* 《儒家倫理新批判》之批判, edited by Guo Qiyong. Wuhan: Wuhan University Press, pp. 1–23.

—2011a. "On Mutual Disclosure of Wrongdoings Among Family Members, Legal Allowance for Nondisclosure, and Their Implications on Legal Reform Today '親親相隱' '容隱制' 及其對當今法治建設的啟迪." In *Critiques of A New Critique of Confucian Ethics*《儒家倫理新批判》之批判, edited by Guo Qiyong. Wuhan: Wuhan University Press, pp. 1–23.

Guo, Qiyong 郭齊勇, ed. 2004. *A Collection of Essays in the Debate on Confucius Ethics* 儒家倫理爭鳴集. Wuhan: Hubei Jiaoyu Chubanshe.

—2011. *Critiques of A New Critique of Confucian Ethics*《儒家倫理新批判》之批判. Wuhan: Wuhan University Press.

Guo, Qiyong 郭齊勇 and Gong Jianping 龔建平. 2004. "The Mutual Non-disclosure of Wrongdoings in the Context of the Governing with Virtue '德治'語境中的'亲亲相隱.'" In *A Collection of Essays in the Debate on Confucius Ethics* 儒家倫理爭鳴集, edited by Guo Qiyong 郭齊勇. Wuhan: Hubei Jiaoyu Chubanshe, pp. 45–62.

Guoyu 國語 (*Speeches from States*). 1998. Nanchang: Jinagxi Gaoxiao Chubanshe.

Hu, Shi 胡適. 1998. "Outline History of Chinese Philosophy 中國哲學史大綱." In *Collected Scholarly Works by Hu Shi: History of Chinese Philosophy* 胡適學術文集: 中國哲學史. Beijing: Zhonghua Shuju.

Huang, Yong. 2005. "A Copper Rule versus the Golden Rule: A Daoist-Confucian Proposals for Global Ethics." *Philosophy East & West* 55.3: 394–425.

—2007. "Introduction." *Contemporary Chinese Thought* 39.1: 3–14.

—2008. "'Why Be Moral?' The Cheng Brothers' Neo-Confucian Answer." *Journal of Religious Ethics* 36.2: 321–53.

—2009. "Neo-Confucian Hermeneutics at Work: Cheng Yi's Philosophical Interpretation of *Analects* 8.9 and 17.3." *Harvard Theological Review* 101: 169–201.

—2010a. "Confucius and Mencius on the Motivation to Be Moral." *Philosophy East and West* 60.1: 65–87.

—2010b. "The Ethics of Difference in the *Zhuangzi*." *Journal of American Academy of Religion* 78.1: 65–99.

—2010c. "The Self-Centeredness Objection to Virtue Ethics: Zhu Xi's Neo-Confucian Response." *American Catholic Philosophical Quarterly* 84.4: 651–92.

—2011. "Two Dilemmas of Virtue Ethics and How Zhu Xi's Neo-Confucianism Avoids them." *Journal of Philosophical Research* 36: 247–81.

—2012. "Toward a Benign Moral Relativism: From Agent/Critics-centered to the Patient-centered." In *Confucianism, Daoism, and Moral Relativism: Wong Responds to Critics*, edited by Xiao Yang and Huang Yong. New York: State University of New York Press.

Huang, Yusheng 黃裕生. 2003. "The Starting Point of a Universal Ethics: Free Individual or Relational Role?" In *A Collection of Essays in the Debate on Confucius Ethics* 儒家倫理爭鳴集, edited by Guo Qiyong 郭齊勇. Wuhan: Hubei Jiaoyu Chubanshe, 938–63.

Hurka, Thomas. 2001. *Virtue, Vice, and Value*. Oxford: Oxford University Press.

Hursthouse, Rosalind. 1999. *On Virtue Ethics*. Oxford: Oxford University Press.

Jingmen Shi Bowuguan 荊門市博物館. 1998. *Bamboo Strips Excavated from the Chu Tombs at Guodian* 郭店楚墓竹簡. Beijing: Wenwu chubanshe.

Kongzi Jiayu 孔子家语 (*Conversations of Confucius's Family*). 2009. Beijing: Beijing Yanshan Chubanshe.

Kongzi Jiyu 孔子集語 (*Collected Sayings of Confucius*). 2002. Ha'erbin: Heilongjian Renmin Chubanshe.

Kraut, Richard. 1989. *Aristotle on the Human Good*. Princeton: Princeton University Press.

Kuang, Yaming 匡亞明. 1990. *A Critical Biography of Confucius* 孔子評傳. Nanjing: Nanjing Daxue Chubanshe (Nanjing University Press).

Kupperman, Joe L. 2008. "Fact and Value in the *Analects*: Education and Logic." In *Educations and Their Purposes*, edited by Roger T. Ames and Peter Hershock. Honolulu: University of Hawaii Press, pp. 405–19.

—2010. "Confucian Civility." *Dao: A Journal of Comparative Philosophy* 9.1: 11–23.

Laozi 老子. In *Annotations and Interpretations of* Laozi 老子校釋. Beijing: Zhonghua Shuju.

Lau, D. C., trans. 1979. *Confucius: The* Analects. Middlesex, England: Penguin Books.

Li, Ling 李零. 2007. *A Homeless Dog: My Reading of the* Analects 喪家狗：我讀論語. Taiyuan: Shanxi Renmin Chubanshe.

Li, Zehou 李澤厚. 1999. *A Contemporary Reading of the* Analects 論語今讀. Hong Kong: Tiandi Tushu.

Liji 禮記 (*The Book of Rites*). In *An Annotated Translation of the* Book of Rites 禮記譯註, by Yang Tianyu 楊天宇. Shanghai: Shanghai Guji Chubanshe.

Liu, Qingping 劉清平. 2004. "On the Confucian Consanguinism in Confucius and Mencius 論孔孟儒學的血亲團體性特征." In *A Collection of Essays in the Debate on Confucius Ethics* 儒家倫理爭鳴集, edited by Guo Qiyong 郭齊勇. Wuhan: Hubei Jiaoyu Chubanshe, pp. 853–87.

Lü's Spring and Autumn 呂氏春秋. 2003. Ha'erbin: Heilongjiang Renmin Chubanshe.

McDowell, John. 1998. *Mind, Value, & Reality*. Cambridge, MA: Harvard University Press.

Mencius. 2005. In *Translation and Annotation of the* Mencius 孟子譯注, by Yang Bojun 楊伯峻. Beijing: Zhonghua Shuju.

Meng, Peiyuan 蒙培元. 1993. *Thought on the Subject in Chinese Philosophy* 中國哲學主體思維. Beijing: Renmin Chubanshe.

—2004. "Human Beings as Emotional Beings." In *A Collection of Essays in the Debate on Confucius Ethics* 儒家倫理爭鳴集, edited by Guo Qiyong 郭齊勇. Wuhan: Hubei Jiaoyu Chubanshe, pp. 455–472.

Midgley, Mary. 1995. *Beast and Man*. London: Routledge.

Mu, Nanke. 2004. "The Original Context of Confucian Classics and Its Methodological Implications 儒家典籍的語境溯源及方法論意義." In *A Collection of Essays in the Debate on Confucius Ethics* 儒家倫理爭鳴集, edited by Guo Qiyong 郭齊勇. Wuhan: Hubei Jiaoyu Chubanshe, pp. 964–71.

Niebuhr, Reinhold. 1960. *Moral Man and Immoral Society*. New York: Scribner's Sons.

Nielsen, Kai. 1989. *Why Be Moral*. Buffalo: Prometheus Books.

Plato. *The Republic*. In *Plato: The Collected Dialogues*, edited by Edith Hamilton and Huntington Cairns. Princeton: Princeton University Press.

Qian, Mu 錢穆. 2001. *Confucius and the* Analects 孔子和論語. Taipei: Lantai Chubanshe.

—2005. *A Biography of Confucius* 孔子傳. Beijing: Sanlian.

—2005a. *A New Interpretation of the* Analects 論語新解. Beijing: Sanlian Shudian.

Ridley, Mark and Richard Dawkins. 1981. "Natural Selection and Altruism." In *Altruism and Helping Behavior: Social, Personality, and Developmental Perspectives*, edited by Philippe Rushton and Richard M. Sorretino. Hillsdale, NJ: Lawrence Erlbaum Associates, pp. 19–40.

Rorty, Richard. 1998. *Truth and Progress: Philosophical Papers*. Cambridge: Cambridge University Press.

Silk, J. B., A. Samuels, and P. Rodman. 1981. "The Influences of Kinship, Rank, and Sex on Affiliation and Aggression between Adult Female and Immature Bonnet Macaques." *Behavior* 78: 111–77.

Sima, Qian 司馬遷. 2008. "Confucius's Family 孔子世家." In *Records of History* 史記, vol. 47. Beijing: Zhonghua Shuju.

—2008a. "Biographies of Han Fei and Laozi." In *Records of History* 史記, vol. 63. Beijing: Zhonghua Shuju.

—2008b. "Biographies of Upright Officials 循吏列傳." In *Records of History* 史記, vol. 119. Beijing: Zhonghua Shuju.

Solomon, David. 1997. "Internal Objections to Virtue Ethics." In *Virtue Ethics: A Critical Reader*, edited by Daniel Statman. Washington, DC: Georgetown University Press, pp. 165–179.

Stocker, Michael. 1997. "The Schizophrenia of Modern Ethical Theories." In *Virtue Ethics*, edited by Roger Crisp and Micahel Slote. Oxford: Oxford University Press, pp. 66–78.

Tang, Junyi 唐君毅. 1991. *On the Sources of Chinese Philosophy: Human Nature* 中國哲學原論:原性篇. Taipei: Xuesheng Shuju.

Toner, Christopher. 2006. "The Self-Centeredness Objection to Virtue Ethics." *Philosophy* 81: 595–617.

Toulmin, Stephen. 1964. *An Examination of the Place of Reason in Ethics*. Cambridge: Cambridge University Press.

Wang, Qingjie. 2010. "Virtue Ethics and Being Morally Moved." *Dao: A Journal of Comparative Philosophy* 9.3: 309–321.

Williams, Bernard. 1971. *Morality: An Introduction to Ethics*. New York: Harper.

—1995. "Replies." In *World, Mind, and Ethics: Essays on the Ethical Philosophy of Bernard Williams*, edited by J. E. J. Altham and Ross Harrison. Cambridge: Cambridge University Press, pp. 185–224.

Wittgenstein, Ludwig. 1958. *Philosophical Investigation*. New York: Macmillan.

Xiaojing 孝經 (*The Book of Filial Piety*). 1996. In *Translation and Annotations of the* Book of Filial Piety 孝經譯注. Beijing: Zhonghua Shuju.

Xu, Fuguan 徐復觀. 1999. *A History of Chinese Theories of Human Nature: The Pre-Qin Period* 中國人性論史:先秦篇. Taipei: Shangwu Yingshuguan.

Xunzi. 1999. In *Library of Chinese Classics: Chinese-English*. Chashang: Hu'nan Renmin Chubanshe & Beijing: Waiwen Chubanshe.

Yang, Bojun 楊伯峻. 1980. *Translation and Annotation of the* Analects 論語譯註. Beijing: Zhonghua Shuju.

Yang, Guorong 楊國榮. 2011. "Metaphysics, Cultivation of Others, Norm, Knowledge, and Value 形上學, 成人, 規範, 知識, 價值." *Philosophical Analysis* 哲學分析 2.5: 42–59.

Yang, Zebo 楊澤波. 2004. "Corruption or Unreasonable Requirement 腐敗還是苛求?" In *A Collection of Essays in the Debate on Confucius Ethics* 儒家倫理爭鳴集, edited by Guo Qiyong 郭齊勇. Wuhan: Hubei Jiaoyu Chubanshe, pp. 92–116.

Ye, Jingzhu 葉經柱. 1977. *Confucius's Moral Philosophy* 孔子的道德哲學. Taibei: Zhongzhong Shuju.

Zhang, Bingnan 張秉楠. 1997. *Confucius* 孔子. Changchun: Jilin Wenshi Chubanshe.

Zheng, Jiadong 鄭家棟. 2004. "The Father–Child Relationship and Its Interpretational Perspective in Traditional Chinese Thought 中國傳統思想中的父子關係及詮釋的面向." In *A Collection of Essays in the Debate on Confucius Ethics* 儒家倫理爭鳴集, edited by Guo Qiyong 郭齊勇. Wuhan: Hubei Jiaoyu Chubanshe, pp. 473–93.

Zhongyong 中庸 (*The Doctrine of the Mean*). 1963. "The Doctrine of the Mean." In *A Source Book in Chinese Philosophy*, trans. and compiled by Wing-Tsit Chan. Princeton: Princeton University Press (translation modified).

—1994. In *Collected Commentaries on the Four Books* 四書章句集註, by Zhu Xi. Taibei: Da'an Chubanshe.

Zhu, Xi 朱熹. 1986. *Classified Sayings of Master Zhu* 朱子語類. Beijing: Zhonghua Shuju.

Zuozhuan 左傳 (*Zuo's Commentary on the Spring and Autumn Annals*). 1990. In *Annotations of* Zuo's Commentary on the Spring and Autumn Annals 春秋左傳注. Beijing: Zhonghua Shuju.

INDEX